"ENTRAPMENT"

Publisher, Ivan S Tuttle
First Edition
Published April 11, 2014
Second Edition
Published August 9, 2014

Contents

Introduction

This book was written about the death, or what society calls a NDE (Near Death Experience), I had back in 1978. At that time in my life I was not living a very good life, I was mixed up in drugs and at 26 years old, my life was spiraling out of control. I made some bad choices for my life back then, but little did I know that my mother would be so instrumental in helping me back.

I went straight to hell when I died. It was a horrible place with people screaming and yelling constantly and begging to get out of hell. Some people had been there for thousands of years and they would beg everyone new being brought into hell asking them to help them get out. Hell was the most horrible place I had ever seen and since that experience, I plan on staying out of. The monsters or demons there in hell and what they do to you unbelievable, you will find out more about them and what hell is like as you read the book.

After being in hell for a little time, I was taken to heaven because of a special promise, which I won't disclose here in the introduction. While in heaven I was met by an angel of God and was told many things, shown things about the future and was told and shown things about heaven.

There are things about heaven I never knew till going there and only people that have gone there before can fully understand. I have had the pleasure of meeting a couple other people that have died and gone to heaven and it is such a pleasure talking with them. It is an experience that very few every really have and I thank God every day for that chance to visit and come back, but I wish I never had to leave. You will read about many of these experiences in the book.

I write in the book about my life at the time this experience happened because I want you to know how I was living, why this experience happened like it did and how come I was spared and allowed to live and come back to life on earth. It is important that you know what it was like for me as a child growing up, the hardships I went through and the relationship I had with my father. Understanding how I grew up and how I ended up dead is very important in understanding why I titled the book, "ENTRAPMENT."

After I came back to life I was scared and afraid to go back to sleep at first because my mind could not comprehend what my spirit had just gone through. The next morning after dying, I went straight to my doctor's consultation office because I needed to know what happened to me. I was rather rattled at first, but as my mind started catching up with what happened to my spirit, I began to calm down and started understanding what happened to me.

Back in 1978, I didn't start writing about what happened to me after I died, because I was not ready to do that at that point in my life and I was told by the angel in heaven that I would be told when to write it. At the end of August, 2013, I was spoken to by the Holy Spirit that now it was time to write and tell about my experience in hell and heaven.

I've never written a book before, had no idea how to write one, I am ADHD and sitting still that long to write a book seemed impossible, but, I did what I was told to do. I can remember so well that day I started writing, I sat down at one end of the sofa and my wife was on the other end, because we have the kind of sofa that each end reclines and has leg rests. I opened up my laptop and began to type, that alone is a sight to see because I have to look at my hands to type, I was never given lessons. I started typing away and what I thought was only about a half hour long, ended up being a little over four hours.

As I finished the first eight pages that first day, I thought that I was done doing what I was supposed to do. Yes, only 8 pages, but I have never written that many pages in my life about anything I have ever done or gone through. I was so proud of those eight pages. I sent it to several friends and asked them what they thought and thank

God, I have friends that tell the truth! Every one of them told me that there were no details in it and questioned me as to why I didn't give details. Well, that started me on the path of writing this book and I figured out that those eight pages would be the rough draft outline of my book.

Because I have never written a book before, I went to the one person that knew has written several books, my pastor Greg Brown of Skyway Church in Goodyear, Arizona. He is a gracious man and met with me and told me how a book should be laid out and about how many words a book should have in it to be a good book. Now let me explain; I only had about six thousand words in what I had written so far and when he told me my book should have at least "twenty-five thousand" words in it, my heart sank. I realized then that I had a lot of work to do!

I came home that afternoon and began to write day after day until I knew that the book was complete and that I had included everything the angel in heaven told me I should have in this book. There are many things that I saw, heard and felt, but there is not enough time to disclose everything yet, but there are a lot of things I saw and experienced that are written about in this book. I hope you enjoy reading it and I pray that this book will "Change Your Life As You Know It Now."

Dedication

I would like to dedicate this book to two very special people in my life, my mother, Helen and my son, Christopher.

My mother Helen, because without her I would still be in hell forever, being tortured for all eternity, thank you mother for your prayers. My mother has prayed for me more than 40,000 times in my lifetime so far.

My son Christopher, because he has been the recipient of the gifts God has given me and has grown into a fine man of God. He is the greatest son a father could ever have. Thank you son for everything!

"ENTRAPMENT"

1

Denial

It was February 1978, and Grand Rapids, Michigan was very cold. There seemed to be an unusual amount of snow that month. We'd just experienced one of the worst winter snow storms in Grand Rapids' history only a few weeks earlier and it seemed like the snow just wasn't going to let up. Grand Rapids, and most of Western Michigan, has something called Lake Effect Snow throughout the winter. Sometimes overnight it would snow an inch or less, while at other times as much as a foot would drop while you were sleeping. This was due to the Lake Effect Snow; something I wasn't used to back in Maryland where I grew up.

I was working selling Oldsmobile's and Hondas at a car dealership there in Grand Rapids, Michigan, and just about every winter morning when I got to work, just like everyone else at the dealership, we had to brush off the cars from the overnight Lake Effect Snow. We would stay bundled up, go outside with a broom in a well gloved hand and start clearing off all the snow. Some mornings it took us an hour or longer to brush off all the snow, and that was usually because when we had deeper Lake Effect Snow the night before the dealership was short handed with more employees calling in sick or coming in late so they didn't have to work at clearing away the snow. However, it was my job to do that, and since I made good money selling cars, I didn't complain.

Honda cars were all front wheel drive back then and it made driving in the snow much easier, so during the winter we sold a lot of Hondas. American car manufacturers were just beginning their movement in producing more front wheel drive vehicles, but Honda was way ahead of the game. On the real snowy days the dealership received a lot of phone calls with people asking questions about the Honda front wheel drive cars; such as, "Would they climb hills better in the snow?" "Would they stop better in the snow?", or "How did the Honda handle on turns in the snow?" And on and on the questions went.

At times several of us salesmen would go out for lunch and take someone's Honda demo out in an area that had a lot of hills, curves, and snow, just to see how well the car actually handled in the snow. One time, a salesman named Manny took a turn too fast, panicked, pulled up on the emergency brake handle, and spun around in a couple of circles resulting in his Honda going off the road. There were four of us in the car with him at the time and together we tried to lift the car up to get it back onto the road, but in the end we had to walk to someone's house about a half mile away and use their phone to call the dealership to tow us out. Since cell phones hadn't yet been invented back then it was either use a payphone or someone's home phone, and since we were out too far away from town and there were no businesses or payphones around, the only option was to look for a friendly resident and request the use of their phone.

Thursday night was here, that meant it was "Ladies Night" at the club and I couldn't wait to get off of work and head to the bars, but first I needed to go home and smoke a joint. I got off work around 6:00 p.m. that night, drove home to my apartment, lit a joint, and got something to eat. Following that, I took a shower and got dressed up for a night of dancing with the ladies. I remember being restless that night because my left leg was bothering me. I thought it was just tight, or maybe I had pulled a calf muscle, so I tried stretching it out. About 8:30 p.m. I left my apartment to head to the nightclub; it was snowing pretty well and the roads were a little slick so I had to really pay attention to my driving that night.

I arrived at the club a little before 9:00 p.m. and did what I normally did; walked around the dance floor and the bar area trying to decide where the best seat would be to observe the ladies as they danced. I found a table kind of off to the side of the dance floor where there was a little more light so not only could I see them, but they could see me, too. Then I ordered a drink and just waited and watched while people began to fill the club. By 9:30 my leg was really bothering me, but I just thought again that my calf muscle was only cramping up on me. I found a few ladies to dance with, but by 11:00 p.m. my leg was throbbing so badly that I sat down and didn't dance anymore. Because I loved disco music, it was really hard to just sit there and watch everyone else dance. There were a couple of ladies that asked me to dance and I turned them down that night, which was unusual for me. But the pain was becoming much worse, and I just knew I couldn't get up and dance. Now I did something I never do. I left around midnight; two hours earlier than usual and by myself. As soon as I got in the door of my apartment I took my shoes and pants off and started trying to massage my left calf. Then I smoked another joint and fell asleep on my sofa.

Friday morning, around 7:30 a.m., I woke up to pain in my left calf. I wondered when the muscle cramp was ever going to relax so that it didn't hurt so badly! Around 8:00 a.m. I called in to work to let them know I might not be coming in because my leg was hurting so much. By 10:00 a.m., an hour after I was supposed to be at work, I decided to go in because I needed a few more sales so I could have more party money for the next few weeks. When I arrived at the dealership I started right off with a customer; it was a man with his wife and two children and he wanted to test drive the little 4 door Honda. Well, that meant I had to get in the back seat next to the two children and there wasn't a whole lot of room for adults in those back seats. We took off going north on the road in front of the dealership and after we went about three miles down the road, my left calf was hurting so badly I had to ask him to pull the car into an apartment parking lot so I could stretch my legs. I told the couple that I had a bad muscle cramp in my calf. I got out of the car and tried walking it off, but it didn't work so I had to ask the man's wife if she would please ride in the back with her children. She did, and we got back to the dealership about ten minutes later. Needless to say, I didn't make a sale there since I had to cut it short with them.

As the pain became more intense I finally left work to go home in order to lie down with my feet elevated; my leg felt better in that position. As soon as I got home, about 12:30 that afternoon, I lit up a joint right away. I mean after all, I wasn't going back to work, so who cares? I remember getting something to eat and then passing out on my sofa again. Around 5:30 that evening I awoke, smoked the rest of the joint, and fixed some dinner. I think it was a TV dinner, you know - lousy, soggy chicken, a vegetable that wasn't identifiable, and something they called dessert. My leg was still bothering me but felt a little better since I had been off of my feet so much, so I decided to go out partying again. This time I called a couple friends of mine; my two party going friends, Mike and Russell. They came over and we smoked some pot together. Mike had some new type of pot from Hawaii he wanted us to try, said it was laced with opium, like Thai-sticks were. WOW! That stuff really had some kick to it; I only took two drags off it and was almost wiped out.

The three of us sat around listening to some music until about 9:00 pm and then decided to go to the club. Before we left, we smoked some more of that Hawaiian weed Mike had brought. I drove my car and Mike and Russell rode together in Russell's car. I don't think either one of us drove much over 25 miles per hour all the way there; for one thing we were too stoned to drive any faster, and with the roads snow covered and icy, driving slow was a good idea.

No matter how stoned I got that night, my leg was killing me and I wasn't much fun. I declined dancing with any of the ladies that asked me to, telling them "My old football injury is acting up and it is too difficult to dance." I received great sympathy points from the girls that night; several of them bought me drinks and sat at my table talking with me, but it was difficult keeping a conversation with them with all the pain I was having in my leg.

We generally partied till the bar closed down around 1:30 to 2:00 in the morning and then hopefully we had company to take with us, but that night I told the guys I had to leave because my leg was hurting so bad. So I left around midnight and drove straight home. Because it was snowing (surprise) I had to drive extra slow and careful. I had come down from smoking the pot and the alcohol buzz was very minor so I was not too impaired; unlike most weekend nights. I arrived home safely, parked in my allotted space at my apartment complex, and walked inside my apartment. By this time the pain was very intense. I couldn't sit, stand, or lie down to make it feel better, so I smoked several bowls of pot until I fell asleep.

I awoke in severe pain around 7:30 the next morning. "What a horrible day this is going to be", I thought. That's when I decided it was time to see a doctor, so I took a shower, got dressed, and started calling around to see if there was a doctor available to see me. I finally found one over by Butterworth Hospital that was open on Saturdays and he told me to come on in.

Around 9:30 a.m. I arrived at the doctor's office and filled out all the required paperwork. Yes, even back then you had to sign your life away before anyone would see you. I can't recall the doctor's name, but I do remember he seemed like a nice guy. I would say he was about fiftyish, tall, medium build with black hair, and kind of graying around his ears. His accent I would place as European, but I am not sure if he was Polish, Ukrainian, or from somewhere else around that region. "Well, Mr. Tuttle, what seems to be your problem?" the doctor asked while looking at the paperwork I had filled out. Before I could respond, though, he continued, "Oh, I see, you are having Charlie horses or leg cramps in your left calf. How old are you?" he asked. "I'm 26, almost 27", I answered. "Well, drop your pants so I can have a look at it" the doctor said. I dropped my pants and the doctor blurted out, "That leg is really swollen!" Then the doctor had me lie flat on my back on his little exam table while he poked at my leg, took measurements of both calves, listened with his stethoscope to something in both legs and then stood up straight and said, "I think you have Thrombophlebitis. It's a blood clot deep within the calf of the leg and it causes swelling like this. How old are you again?" I told him 26, and he asked me, "Do you smoke a lot of cigarettes?" I replied "I smoke a pack or two a day depending on how many customers I have to wait on each day." The conversation then turned quite serious as the doctor explained to me what could happen if I didn't receive treatment for the Thrombophlebitis right away. He even called the hospital for me and told them I would be coming right over; but I had other ideas as I wasn't ready yet to do that.

I left the doctor's office thinking that blood clots were for old people, not someone my age. I thought that maybe if I just elevated my leg for the rest of the weekend that it would go away, so I bypassed the hospital and went straight home. There I took a couple of pillows from the bedroom into the living room and propped my leg up on the sofa and sat back and watched TV all day.

A young lady I knew, whom I will call Jennifer, came over to see if she could help any. Jennifer was very nice looking, about 20 years old with dark, nearly black hair and a nice figure. Besides that, she worked as a nurse's aide so I thought maybe she would be a good person to have around for a couple days. Now that was against my normal policy to have a girl stay for more than one night, but I needed help and she was really kind and understanding.

Jennifer fixed me dinner that night; in fact she went shopping and bought some food with her own money and made us a meal of hamburgers and macaroni and cheese. It was good to have someone wait on me like this; I kind of liked it, plus my leg was feeling a little bit better just leaving it elevated like that. Jennifer and I sat there and watched TV together and smoked some pot, and around 10:00 o'clock we went to bed. I fell asleep somewhat quickly that night; the pot seemed to hit me pretty hard and quick. I woke up sometime around 3:00 to 3:30 in the morning with my left leg feeling rather numb. It felt as if someone had stuck a thousand pins and needles in it, kind of like how your arm or leg would feel after it falls asleep and it starts to wake up again. I got up to use the bathroom and I thought I was going to pass out from the pain in my left leg, but I hobbled on into the bathroom and then back into bed and fell asleep again.

In the morning I woke up feeling somewhat refreshed, with the pain not nearly as bad as it had been so I got up and fixed Jennifer and me some cereal and toast for breakfast. It was Sunday and February, so there was not much to watch on TV, but together we sat and watched everything from church programs to cartoons, and reruns of other old shows. Then about 6:00 pm that evening I was feeling really good so I took Jennifer out for some pizza. We went to Pizza Hut and got a large pepperoni pizza and a pitcher of root beer. Yes, root beer; I've never liked the taste of beer with pizza. We even played a game called 'Pong' while we ate our pizza. I think we were there for at least two hours, and for the first time in quite a while my leg wasn't killing me.

We got home around 8:45 that night, smoked some pot, watched TV and finally went to bed around 11:00 pm. During the night while I was sleeping my leg started to swell up like it had previously. The throbbing woke me up around 5:00 in the morning and it hurt worse than ever before. Every time my heart would beat it felt like my leg was going to explode. I couldn't fall back to sleep so I fixed and ate some cereal for breakfast, then woke up Jennifer so she could go to her home to get ready for work. I walked around in my apartment for a little while, then took a shower and got ready to go to work myself.

If I remember correctly, I got to the dealership that morning about 8:00 a.m.; before any of the managers or other sales people. The service people, parts department employees, and the receptionist, were the first to have already arrived at work. The showroom doors were still locked, so I went in through the service entrance. I stood by the receptionist's desk for a few minutes talking to the girl working there, and then I decided to go out and sweep some snow off of the cars on the lot. As crazy as this may sound, being out in the cold weather actually made my leg hurt less. I cleaned off two long rows of cars, maybe twenty cars in the front row and fifteen or so cars in the next row, before anyone else showed up for work.

My manager came in around 8:50 a.m. and asked me who had swept the cars off so soon. Well, I was pretty proud to tell him that I had. After that, I went to my desk and started calling prospective customers I had talked with over the past few months to see if there was anything I could do to help them make a decision on getting a new car anytime soon. December wasn't a bad month, but January liked to have killed me in sales; only twelve cars sold the entire month. That was a whole lot less than the fifteen to twenty-five or so cars a month I was used to selling! I had to make more sales despite the pain in my leg, or I was going to run out of party money.

Later that morning, close to lunch time, my leg started hurting so bad that nothing helped; not sitting, standing or lying down. I had to do something about it, and soon. I went to lunch by myself, grabbed a sandwich at this little hole in the wall place, and sat in my car eating it. Then I got this great idea that since my leg felt better being in the cold, I would get ice and put it around my leg. So I drove to my apartment, but unfortunately, like most bachelors back then, I never filled the ice trays so I had to get back in the car and go to the 7-11 for a bag of ice. Funny, I can still remember I only paid $.49 for a 20 lb. bag of ice. Fifteen minutes later I was sitting at the apartment on my sofa with my left leg propped up on a pillow folded over, and two plastic bags full of ice on my leg with an old ace bandage wrapped around them to keep them from slipping off.

2

Back to My Childhood

Somehow, I just couldn't figure out how I had gotten this far off course in life, not financially, but my walk with the Lord. You see, when I was a kid around eight years old, I accepted Jesus into my life and got baptized shortly after that. Then when I was ten years old, I received the baptism of the Holy Spirit. All through my preteen and teenage years, I tried to serve the Lord. Back then I was made fun of sometimes because of it, but I did have my friends at church, so that made things better at times.

One of my best friends at church during those years was Nick Tavani. Nick was one of the smartest people I knew, plus he played the piano. Nick became president of our CA (Christ Ambassadors) group; the CA was a group of teenagers from our church in Forestville, Maryland, which was an Assemblies of God church. Nick's father was a science professor; I believe at the University of Maryland. I looked up to Nick and his family, they had a great walk with the Lord and Nick was so talented and smart. Nick often helped me understand some things in life that I was unaware of in my small world.

Nick accepted me, and I guess you could say he didn't judge me the way some other kids did. Oh, he might have thought I was odd, but he still accepted me. Nick wasn't real coordinated, he was just real smart, so he taught me some things and I taught him some things about football; not rules or anything, but how to play. I remember one time we were over at a school close to his house called Francis Scott Key Junior High and some of us guys from church were playing touch football and somehow I got a nasty cut above my eye. That was the first time in my life I had to get stitches, although only three of them, but the shot to numb it was worse than the stitches!

You see, my childhood wasn't the best of life. I had a father who beat me a lot, but I also had a mother who loved me and prayed for me daily. My father was a bricklayer, a big and strong man that worked all the time trying to get ahead in life. He would work as many as three different jobs at the same time to make sure we had food on the table and a roof over our heads. As a bricklayer, he would work his regular eight to ten hour days, then come home, shower and go do a side job. Additionally, every Thursday night he would go to the local Acme Supermarket in Suitland, Maryland and mop their floors. They let my father do this, and instead of pay they compensated him with all the day old bread, pastries, and pies the store had in stock. My mom and dad would put all the goodies in the freezer out in the side enclosed porch at our house on Woodland Road in Morningside, Maryland.

I guess I should tell you, I had three sisters and one brother, but with my brother being twelve years younger than me he didn't get a lot of those pastries and pies! I can remember coming home after school around 3:30 p.m. and going out to the freezer and getting something to eat like cupcakes or Twinkies. Once in a while I would actually go out there and take a whole pie with me as I darted out to the woods behind the house to eat it, and yes, I would eat the whole thing! Even though I was the skinniest kid around, I ate a lot.

As a kid I was so skinny, I was always being invited by other parents into their home to have something to eat. I can remember one time after eating at one house I walked out the door and went about a block down the street and another neighbor lady invited me in to eat some food there. Now to top it off, as I left that house, I didn't get three doors down when another mother asked me to come in and eat there. I had three big meals in less than an hour. Now I was full, and I do mean full, but I was so skinny everyone thought I wasn't getting enough to eat at home, so they tried to fatten me up.

I have since been diagnosed as ADHD and for those of you who are confused about ADHD, let me explain. ADHD does not mean you are a bad person, it just means your brain is going faster than most and you get bored quickly with everything at normal speed, so you can't sit still and you want to check everything out in life. That's what gets us into trouble! The problem us people have with real ADHD is that many doctors now diagnose every kid that has a problem and claim it is ADHD, and they put them on drugs to try and control it. Many of the children diagnosed today actually have parents with short fuses and they have no idea how to discipline their child or pay attention to them. The real problem is that the parents have an "Attention Deficit Disorder;" not paying enough Attention causing a Deficit in in their relationship with their children and causing that relation to be in Disorder! This puts all of us in a group of badly behaved kids, which we weren't. I didn't try to be bad; I always tried to do the right thing. I just lost interest in things quickly and wanted to know what's next.

As a kid I would sit in class and watch the teacher as she taught us stuff so slowly that it felt like I was watching paint dry, so I would look out the window of my class and dream about being in the woods across the playground. I would dream about being Davy Crockett or Daniel Boone, but the problem was, I was in the classroom and sometimes, while daydreaming, I would be moving around in my seat because my mind was so active with thought. When the teacher would notice that I was looking out the window and fidgeting around in my chair she would ask me a question about whatever subject we were doing and I had no idea what she was talking about.

This got me sent to the principal's office a lot. Everything was just too slow for me.

Back when I was growing up, no one understood a child that couldn't sit still or keep quiet; they didn't know about ADHD so we were just considered "Bad Kids." I just couldn't help it, I hated school and wanted to go play out in the woods; become Daniel Boone or Davey Crockett. School was so boring to me, too slow; I wanted to just go do something, anything but sit there in class. This behavior was also displayed at home, where the consequences were much worse.

At school, the worst thing that could happen was Mrs. Solbeleski, the principal, would use the paddle on me. She had broken a few of them on me before but she only swatted me three times at the most. Now, at home it was much worse because my father would beat me with a belt. Remember, he was a big, strong man; a bricklayer. He knew how to swing that belt and fifteen to twenty lashes was common. Most of my childhood I had welts all over my behind, my legs and my back, and sometimes the welts would bleed. My father had such anger towards me; which I eventually found out why and I will explain later in the book. Some days he would come home from work and if I did not get out before he came home, he would beat me with the belt asking me, "What did you do wrong today? I know you did something, what was it?" I finally got wise to that and as soon as I saw him take his belt off I made up stuff that I had done wrong, even though I really hadn't misbehaved, just so my dad would stop beating me so much. If I waited until he started beating me, I might get ten or fifteen whacks with the belt and then admit to something and get ten or fifteen more whacks with the belt, but if I just made something up, he would only hit me about fifteen to twenty times.

To make matters worse for me as a kid, I had been born with a deformed left hand and arm. So not only did I get abuse from my dad, but at school most of the kids made fun of me and it seemed like someone always wanted to beat me up or start a fight with me after school. I was not a violent kid, but I got tired real quick of kids hitting me and making fun of me, so I stood up to them. I may have been skinny, but I was real strong. I hated fighting because it reminded me of my dad and how it felt to get beat, so I tried everything to get out of a fight, but when I had no choice, I wasn't going to lose. You see, if I lost a fight and my dad found out about it, he would whip me so hard and tell me I wasn't man enough and other hurtful things like that.

When I was just nine years old, one day right after school on the playground, I punched a kid in a fight so hard it knocked him out. I thought I killed him because his eyes rolled back in his head and he just went down like a limp dishrag. I was scared and took off running fast. I ran to my house about a half mile away and told my mother what happened; how this kid had started a fight with me and how I hit him and I thought I killed him. My mother grabbed her keys and we got in the car and she drove as fast as she could back to my school. When we got there the school nurse was just bringing this kid around with smelling salts. Thank God I didn't kill him, he was only knocked out. For a few weeks after that fight no kids picked on me because they were afraid that I would knock them out too. Finally, I enjoyed a few weeks of peace in my life; no one to fight and I could walk home without fear.

This bears repeating - I really didn't want to fight and never started a fight in my life. I always made the other person swing at me or hit me first, with just one exception. There was one time I was egged on to starting a fight with a kid from across the street from me; I sucker punched him and he wouldn't fight. I felt so bad and ran home, up to my room and started crying. Later that day I went over to his house and apologized to him and asked for his forgiveness. I couldn't believe that I actually hit a kid for no reason. As far as I was concerned, I was no better than my father after doing that.

During Junior High School I did not dress out for PE a lot because I was so embarrassed about the welts all over my back and legs. I didn't want all the other kids thinking I was a bad person, so I hid this very well throughout seventh and eighth grade. Then one day when I was fourteen I finally stood up to my dad and he quit beating me.

I can remember the day very well; it was a rainy Sunday morning late in November and I just happened to walk downstairs at the wrong time. My father was upset because there was not enough wood in the wood box by the fireplace for his liking. He was standing in our family room next to the fireplace, so he saw me when I reached the bottom of the steps coming into the room. He said something about getting more wood in the firewood box, but I didn't know he was talking to me. My dad called me over to him and slapped me right across the face and it nearly knocked me out. As I was falling back from the hit I could hear my father yelling at me about putting some wood in the box. After I hit the floor and started to regain myself, I told him that I was in my church clothes and asked him if I could get more wood after church. This just upset him all the more that I would try to reason with him; I mean after all, no one ever questioned him. He wanted more pieces of wood in the firewood box right then and there and expected my immediate obedience at his command. Next thing I knew, my dad had picked me up in the air with one hand as he hit me in the chest with his other hand. It knocked the breath out of me and stunned me for a few moments. As I got up this time, I was very mad and had had enough. I shook my fist at my father and said, "You hit me one more time and I will kill you!" I can picture my father's face right now as it went from anger to laughter. It started with a small little grin, then went to a little bit of a chuckle, and then grew to an all-out hearty laugh. "So you are going to take me on?" my father asked with a huge smile across his face. I said, "Yes! I am not going to let you keep hitting me like this anymore. I would rather die trying than to allow you to keep hitting me!" The next thing I knew, he walked away and said, "Go to church." After that my father never laid a hand on me again.

High school was really different for me. I was rather timid back then and kept mostly to myself, though I did allow a few kids from church to get a little close to me. I became so shy in my high school years that I only talked to just a few people in school. I did have a girlfriend named Debbie and back then it was such an innocent type of love; what some call "Puppy Love." Holding hands was a big deal back in the 60's and to kiss a girl was about as far as you would ever go out of respect for her and because you knew anything further was wrong. It didn't last long, but it was my first and I have great clean memories!

Now don't get me wrong, I wasn't a perfect kid back then; actually, I was pretty messed up. With all that my father put me through and the harassment from other kids and all the teachers and adults thinking I was a bad kid growing up, I was very insecure. I made a lot of mistakes too, and never really knew what the right thing was to do in many situations. I was always afraid that I wasn't smart enough to be around certain people; in fact, anyone my age or older. I believed there was something wrong with me because, even my own father rejected me as a child. I didn't find out until my early twenties that I actually have a pretty high IQ of 136.

Because I was pretty much a loner in high school, I used to listen to music a lot. I had a little transistor radio and we had a Hi/Fi and turntable console at home. I could sing pretty well, but was too shy to get up in front of people by myself. However, I enjoyed singing in the church and the school choir. Even though I was made fun of in high school I still loved my music. Music was something that I didn't just hear, I felt it, too. I loved music!

My family had moved to Upper Marlboro, Maryland when I was fourteen and back then that was considered country. Across the street from my house there was a huge tobacco field and a big barn where they hung the tobacco to dry. The actual farmer lived about two miles or so away from the barn, so he couldn't see the barn from his house. I used to love to go over there and climb up in the loft area of the barn when it rained. There was something about listening to the rain hit that tin roof that just kind of relaxed me. There even were a few times I actually fell asleep.

Living out in the country did present me with a few problems because we now were about fifteen miles from church and at least seventeen miles from the high school I wanted to attend. Just before I had turned fifteen my father had a heart attack and couldn't work anymore. Now I needed to find a way to and from church on Friday nights, because that's when our youth group met, and try to find a way to get to Suitland High; the school where my friends from church went, too. The school I was supposed to go to was even further out in the country and I knew no one there. Besides being too young to drive, I couldn't afford insurance for me to drive our car or truck, so I learned to hitchhike. It started one day when I wanted to go ice skating with the youth group and the only way I could go was if I could find a ride. Well, no one was going to drive way out in the country to pick me up, but I told my mother they were. I told her they were going to meet me at the store about a half mile down the road. So I walked out the front door, got around the curve in the road so no one could see me from my house and stuck out my thumb. I mean after all, I had seen them do it on TV programs and in the movies, so why not. It was kind of scary but I got a ride right away and he dropped me off on Pennsylvania Avenue, about three blocks away from church. After that, I hitchhiked all over the place; including every day to Suitland High School which was about seventeen miles from my home.

After high school I went to a Bible College up in Brooklin, Maine, called Faith School of Theology. It was very small, and like it said it was a faith school. I didn't have the money to attend, but I was accepted anyway and they allowed me to earn my way through by working for them on their farm. Someone had given the college a dairy farm and the first thing that needed to be done was to clean out the stalls. Wow, that was fun… not! Then we had to put up electric fencing around ten acres. Being that I was the guy from the city, a few of the country guys decided I was the lucky one who got to test out the electric fence we put up. They assured me what I was doing was the safest way to check an electric fence. (I'm sure you already know where this is going.) I was told to get a long piece of grass; kind of like a stalk wheat grows on, and put it between my teeth only and then tap it on the fence. They told me that because my teeth were insulated the electricity wouldn't flow through them and that the stalk of grass would spark but nothing would happen to me.

I found the longest piece of grass like a wheat stalk that I could find; almost a foot long. I placed that stalk of grass in my mouth between my teeth, making sure my tongue didn't touch it and moved close to the fence. I waited till someone turned on the power to the fence and then I proceeded to move even closer. Now about six inches away from the fence on all fours, I waited for someone to tell me it was okay to check it. Finally the guy standing behind me said, "Go ahead, tap it and let us know if you see a spark." Of course I didn't know that everyone was standing back behind me just to watch what I was about to do. I was actually feeling honored that they chose me to be the one to test it! I looked very carefully at the stalk of grass as I lowered my head down towards the electric wire so I could see the spark. Wham! I felt like someone just kicked me in the teeth as my whole mouth felt like it was going to explode and my entire body felt the electricity flowing through it. I jumped backwards, fell to the ground, and rolled on my back just in time to see all the other guys falling down too; but they were falling down from laughter. I almost peed my pants; it hurt that bad and I had never been shocked like that before.

Putting that incident to the side, I enjoyed going to college there. I was taught about public speaking by the President of the college. I can remember him calling me out in class and having me say the word "Obadiah." He made me stand up and say it out loud; I had to fill the whole room up with my voice. Now, as I said earlier, I was very shy back then and afraid to speak in public, but I loved the Lord and wanted to preach. Our instructor worked with me and within a few weeks I was over my fear and ready to preach.

This school was great as it had connections with churches all over Maine that would allow students to preach. I went to one church outside of Bangor, Maine, and stayed there with the pastor and his wife during a Thanksgiving break. I was there to work for my stay, which meant I got to preach. My first sermon ever, I got to preach was that Sunday morning and it was on Romans 12:20... On the contrary: "If your enemy is hungry, feed him; if he is thirsty, give him something to drink. In doing this, you will heap burning coals on his head."

Now this was an old church and the platform you stood on to preach was kind of like a stage, but it was made of hardwood with no carpeting on it and underneath it was hollow; very hollow. Every step you took on it echoed throughout the building. I was very nervous as it was my first time being responsible to preach and only eighteen years old, so I kind of rocked back and forth tapping my feet a lot while I was preaching, and I guess that made more noise than my preaching. I had someone come up to me after the service and tell me that next time try to keep my feet still so they could hear the sermon. I was embarrassed, but it didn't stop me. I loved the Lord so much back then.

Then on one trip home I met a girl who got my attention quick; she was not a Christian, but she was so darn cute. We fell in love, or what I thought was love within my two week stay at home and she begged me not to leave her to go back to college. She convinced me I could make better money doing something other than preaching. She thought I would be perfect for sales and she got me a job at the GEM (Government Employee Membership) store she worked at. Her name was Lynn and she worked in the pharmacy at the GEM store. To make a long story short, that is why I left college and that was when I slipped up and walked away from the Lord. Boy, when I make a mistake, I usually make a big one!

3

Blood Clot

Now back to 1978 and my problem at hand. My health wasn't in the best condition because I would stay up for days on end partying using different drugs to keep me awake. Okay, by this time I knew I had a problem with my left leg and it needed to be taken care of, but I hated going to a doctor's office and questioned who knew what was really wrong with my leg. Were they going to operate on it, how would they get the blood clot out, if there was one? The first doctor I went to had wanted me to go to the hospital right away as he thought I had Thrombophlebitis; a deep blood clot in the calf of the leg. Of course I didn't take his advice to go to the hospital because I wanted to keep partying, and besides that, I was young and invincible, right? So I kept up my lifestyle for a few more days until it got so bad I couldn't walk, sit, or sleep, because of the pain and swelling. Then finally I went to the emergency room at Butterworth Hospital there in Grand Rapids, Michigan.

That night they did some tests on me, measured both legs etc., and believed I had a pretty good size blood clot in my left leg and I had to be hospitalized right away. There I was, only 26 years old and I had something that my grandfather should have; not someone my age. How do they fix this problem? Do they operate on me or what? Finally a doctor walked into my little emergency room draped in area and proceeded to tell me that he indeed believed that I have a blood clot in my leg and that it needed to be treated right away or I could die from it. First they were going to put me in a room and try to stabilize my blood from being so thick, and in order to do that I would need to be off my feet for a few days. Part of the process required them to put me on blood thinners and other medications to thin out my blood and get the swelling down. I thought, this is great; they will fix it in in a day or two and send me back home. After all, I still had some partying to do. Not so quick.

The doctors checked me into the hospital but right off there was a problem. I am highly allergic to Iodine, the substance used in the IVP dye they needed to inject me with to look at the clot in my leg. There was a new Doctor of Radio Active Treatments at the hospital and he thought of another way to see the blockage. He wanted to do a "Radioactive Retrograde Uptake" on me, something innovative back in 1978. At that time, the ultra sound wasn't perfected enough to look for blood clots in your legs.

They took me into this room where they had this big round piece of equipment, about three feet in diameter that had two supporting arms holding it up in the air and a table positioned under it. They were able to move this around with ease like a robot. They laid me down on the table beneath this machine and injected my right leg with this radioactive serum and they moved this big round device over my leg as they watched behind some type of monitor. I could see the monitor and all I saw were hundreds of little dots moving up what must have been my leg. Then they injected it into my left leg. This time as I watched the monitor, I didn't see near as many dots going up my leg; this is the leg they believed I had a clot in. The doctor came over to me and said something like, "We believe that your left leg has a very deep clot in it. We only counted x amount of whatever coming up your leg." He was talking about the radioactive material going up through my leg. The doctors talked amongst themselves and then let me know that the best treatment for me was to remain in bed while they thinned my blood out, and that I needed to wear some kind of stocking type material on my right leg, the one without the clot, in order to equal out the pressure in my legs so my blood would flow better.

They wheeled me into my room, put me in bed and then put this stocking type thing on my leg, put an IV in me, shot me full of some stuff and instructed me that I couldn't get out of bed for any reason. There I was; only 26 years old, full of life, Mr. Party Man, and I had to stay in bed. Talk about being depressed. After about an hour lying in bed, I had to use the restroom. I pressed the red little buzzer button and a nurse came into the room and asked, "What can I do for you?" I let her know I had to use the restroom and she said, "Number one or number two?" I about died laughing when she asked me that. I thought, do I look like I am five years old? Anyways, I told her "number two", and she said, "Wait right there, I'll be right back." She came back in the room with a little bed pan, handed it to me with a roll of toilet paper, pulled the curtain around my bed and said, "Buzz me when you are finished." Right, I am going to do 'WHAT' in this pan and then have you come back in this nice smelling room to take this from me, like it's some kind of GIFT or something?

Needless to say, I had a lot of growing up to do in a very short time. Being in a hospital at 26 and not being able to get out of bed opened me up to a lot of new challenges. I will say that the nurses and Candy Stripers were some of the nicest people I had ever met and they were extremely helpful. A couple of them were even downright cute! I went through a lot of embarrassing moments during my stay, like the bed pan issue and then having to get bathed in bed by strangers. I wasn't sure if I was being treated like a baby, or like an elderly nursing home patient.

Being a smoker at the time, I needed a cigarette and I couldn't get my friends to come into the hospital to bring me any - some friends. After about eight hours of no cigarettes I was going crazy so whenever someone walked past my door I would ask them if they had any cigarettes. Finally one guy did and he brought one into my room. I lit it up and took in a couple of deep drags before nurse 'Crachett' came in my room and read me the riot act about my room being a non-smoking room. You see, back in the 70's there were smoking and non-smoking rooms in hospitals, restaurants, airplanes and just about anyplace else that was public. I asked her to please change my room and she argued with me telling me, "The doctor wanted you in a non-smoking room because he believes smoking causes blood clots." I begged her to please put me in a smoking room. "I can't get out of bed or anything else and I can't smoke and you don't want to see me get like I get when I can't have a cigarette!" I really felt like I was in prison at the time, couldn't do this, couldn't do that. I was pleasantly surprised when she came back in my room and told me that she was moving me down the hall to a smoking room!

I was happy then; I got to get up out of the bed and move to a new room. Well, not exactly; the nurse and an orderly came into my room and pushed my bed all the way down the hall to my new room. I thought for sure I was going to be able to at least get a wheelchair ride, but, oh no, I had to stay in bed while they wheeled the whole bed down there. So I got into my new room but I didn't have it to myself like the last room. There was a guy in there that looked to me to be about as old as Methuselah. His white hair was kind of yellow with smoking all those years and to be honest, it didn't smell too good in the room either. I tried to start a conversation with the guy, "So how long have you been in this joint?" I asked trying to sound cool. He kind of rolled onto his left side facing me and answered, "Cough, cough, cough, cough, hack, hack. Twenty one days so far. Cough, cough." I noticed he was smoking Lucky Strikes and all I could think of was, boy if he only smoked filtered cigarettes he wouldn't be that bad off. His voice was old and shaky sounding; very dry and hoarse.

Later that day I found out my new roommate's name was Bob; he was only 55 and he had something called COPD, Emphysema, and lung cancer as well as a whole host of other problems. We only had one TV in the room and Bob didn't seem to care what I watched on it most of the time, except he wanted to see the news twice a day because he wanted to know what the weather was going to be. I couldn't help thinking that this guy is never going to be out in it again, so what did it matter, but he loved to see how much snow we were getting. It was February in Grand Rapids, Michigan, and we got a lot of snow that winter; that "Lake Effect Snow" which could dump up to a foot of new snow overnight.

I learned that Bob used to drive a snowplow for the county so that's why he loved to watch the weather because he wanted to know how much snow we were getting. Bob started talking more on my second day with him; he told me how much fun he had plowing through the new snow, how it made him feel like he was doing something to help people. He talked about some of the big storms he had to plow through back in the 60's and some more recent ones in the 70's as well. It was difficult to understand him much of the time because he spoke so softly with his raspy voice and then all the coughing and hacking he did.

On day three doctors came in to visit Bob, pulled the curtain around Bob's bed and told him they were moving him to a nursing home, not too far away from the hospital. Bob seemed rather irritated at the doctors that morning because the doctors seemed to be beating around the bush about Bob's prognosis. Finally, I could hear Bob ask, "So tell me Doc, how long do I got?" It seemed like the doctor was never going to answer him as he said, "Bob, (very long pause) it's not much longer, maybe a month or so." The room became very quiet and after what seemed to be an eternity Bob said, "Thank you." The doctor didn't say much after that and then pulled back the curtain from around Bob's bed and left the room. Bob was on his right side staring out the window. I didn't say anything to him; I figured I would just let him be.

About an hour or so later a nurse and a couple other hospital employees came into the room and talked with Bob for a few minutes and then put him in a wheelchair and took him away. Bob did say goodbye to me and I told him good luck as they wheeled him out of my hospital room. For the next two days, I had the room to myself.

I think it was a Monday when I got a new roommate. His name was an odd one I don't think I had ever heard before, like Daradiesh or something like that, but he said, "just call me Adam," so I did. Adam was from Lebanon and he had been in a bad car accident, broke some ribs, his left arm, and his right leg in two places. We talked over the next week or so about many things. He explained that he came to the U.S. as a student going to college and decided to stay here after that. I think Adam was in his middle 30's at that time. He told me very few things about his home country, except that he loved it growing up there. He talked of how the weather was so much nicer, and how he used to swim a lot in the Mediterranean Sea, and that the water was so clear there. We didn't share a lot in common other than the fact that we both smoked. He smoked some kind of Turkish cigarettes and let me have one once. I about died trying to smoke it.

Every day the nurses would come into my room first thing in the morning and check my vital signs, give me a shot of Heparin, a blood thinner, and then within about thirty minutes or so I would get my breakfast; or what was supposed to be breakfast.

Two weeks after I arrived, with no drugs or alcohol for those two weeks, I was finally getting released from the hospital. I couldn't wait to get home and light up a joint. They released me about 4:00 o'clock in the afternoon and I got home about 5:00. The first thing I did was light up a joint and smoked it. After that I got something to eat and watched some TV, then smoked some more pot and around 9:30 that night I felt tired and went to bed. My new girlfriend at the time, Jennifer, was staying there with me while I recovered, and she wondered why I was going to bed so early, but for some reason, I was exhausted that night and had to go to bed. Usually I stayed up till at least midnight most of the time.

4

Going to Hell

Around 11:20 that night, I was woken up by something or someone grabbing my left wrist and holding on to it very tight; pulling me right up out of my body. I turned around to see my lifeless body just lying there. I was shocked and kept trying to break free from this horrible thing. I even tried to turn the light on in the room to no avail; my hand went right through the wall. This thing had a death grip on my wrist and I could not get free. I looked around at everything in the room just trying to think of a way to escape when all of a sudden we started to move through space and time into this horrible darkness. We moved so fast that time didn't matter, and where it took me was the most horrific place I had ever seen, heard, or smelled. I could hear people screaming; at first the sound was way off in the distance, but within seconds the screams were so loud it was as if they were coming from right beside me. The shrieks were beyond anything I have ever heard before, and the stench was indescribably repulsive. The sense of hopeless I felt emanating in this place was totally overwhelming.

The realization finally hit me that I was in hell. No, this was not a dream, and it was not a drug induced hallucination. I was dead and I was in hell. All hope and expectation of life was gone. The evil spirit that had ahold of me had begun laughing at me. It was incredibly grotesque looking and had the strength of a hundred men. As I heard the screams and shrieks of the people there I could feel their pain; in a way considerably beyond what we typically feel here on earth. Our earthly minds and bodies cannot begin to understand or exist with that type of pain. The heat there became unbearable, although I didn't ever see actual flames.

Why was I in hell and I thought; what did I do to deserve this? I remembered having given my heart to the Lord when I was about eight years old; I even went to Bible College for a little while. I didn't hurt anyone or kill anybody, so why was I in hell? Then I realized that the answers didn't really matter because I knew there was no escape and I was trapped there forever; and I do mean forever.

What I didn't realize at first is that I was still moving down towards the center of hell. I wasn't quite there yet; I had only been on the outskirts of hell. All the while, the demon continued to laugh at me with the most hideous sound my ears had ever heard. The best way I can describe it is like in the movies where someone pretends to be the devil or a demon and they talk or yell with that deep, echoing, reverb type of voice. Well, it is even worse than that. And as this demon took me deeper into hell the smell got so terrible that it permeated my whole being, and the sounds of people screaming literally pierced my being. However, I still tried fighting this evil spirit that had me, and I was screaming like the rest of the people there. I could still feel that insufferable heat coming up from below me, too.

Though words seem utterly inadequate in trying to explain this experience, I will try my best to convey to you the hopelessness and horrifying feelings one has when they're in hell. People were all around me. I bumped into some, and they were screaming as loud as they could and cursing God and yelling at me to please tell their children or other loved ones that hell is for real. They knew it was useless, yet they still screamed and cried out in pain. The pain and anguish there is beyond any suffering you have ever known; it literally engulfs your whole being. Kind of like the worst toothache or headache you have ever had times a thousand and it is throughout your whole being. Imagine falling from an airplane at 35,000 feet up and you have no parachute and nothing but concrete below to land on. You know you are going to die. Well, that hopeless feeling you have going all the way down to certain death; that is what hell is like times ten thousand. There is so much more I could tell you about hell, more ways to try and describe the despair, agony, and suffering, but what it all comes down to is this. Just understand, once you are in hell, it is too late to ask God into your life.

It's too late to change your ways or to send a message to others about how awful hell really is. Trust me; you are not going to be running around with your pals partying in hell. You are going to be in total darkness and hopelessness with no chance for escape.

This heinous thing that had ahold of me was taking me further down, and as I felt the heat getting hotter I began to scream as loud as I could. I cried out to God but felt it didn't matter. I thought He wouldn't answer my prayers now that I was dead; I'd had that choice while I was alive. Nothing I could do had any meaning now; I was nothing and felt nothing but complete hopelessness. It was dark and frightening. People were still yelling at me as I passed by them. They screamed "Get me out of here, please!" Most seemed to be locked in place by something unseen; it was too dark for me to tell, but as I moved past them I could see that they could not move. They just grabbed me and tried desperately to hold onto me.

In this state of being, you don't have a body of the type you had when you were alive in your earthly body, but you do have a body. It's difficult to explain in words. You feel pain, and you see and hear everything with perfect vision and hearing. But the pain in hell is unbelievably worse than anything on earth. At least with earthly pain when it gets too bad you can pass out and escape from it, but not in hell. If you get a cut in the flesh, it only hurts where you got cut, but in hell if you cut your finger it hurts throughout your whole being.

I'm sure I have not adequately described the creatures in hell; what they looked like, smelled like, and what they did. There were some creatures that were very big, about ten or twelve feet tall and they were very grotesque with rotted flesh and a smell that matched. Many of them had long, disfigured arms and legs and they were so strong that they could rip you in half. Yet there were others that seemed to just slither around like huge snakes. I could see many of them going to the center of hell and heading back to earth. I just assumed they were being instructed on what to do by Satan himself and they were returning to earth to do it.

Some of these beasts were creatures of deception; they would go enter a body in order to possess it. Usually that would be a very pretty woman or handsome man who then would entice someone to have sex with them. These same demonic spirits would also get people to believe in things like fortune telling, horoscopes, mind reading, etc. These evil spirits would actually work in people with these gifts, though in actuality they were really just well-planned guesses as they have had thousands of years to learn all about people. The twists and turns these demon spirits would do to people and the lies they led them to believe were purposefully deceptive.

People do not realize that many things on earth have demonic beginnings; like stories about vampires, werewolves, white magic, witches, trolls, and ogres. Even the movies where there are supposed to be good witches and warlocks that fight evil come from a demonic background as well. As well as those things you should know that video games that have extreme violence, murder, extra lives when you battle evil forces and the like, all have a demonic presence in them. I don't understand why people are so blind to this today, but that, too, is a trick of the devil. There is no doubt in my mind that some people will get this far in my book and stop reading it because it will offend them or they will think I am crazy, and that is what the devil would want so that he can continue to deceive and control people.

Parents, wake up! This happened to me back in 1978 and I was able to see these types of games before they were ever even invented or released. There is no time after you die, it is forever and you are leading your children straight to hell by letting them play these games! Just look back at kids from the 60's and 70's and then look at the kids in the 80's and 90's and you can see the difference. Now look at the kids today, there is very little communication with them, they are always playing these games and ignoring their parents. You go to church and your children do, too, and they seem like good kids, but there is a deep, dark side you do not know about your own children when you allow them access to these things. I understand your kids keep telling you that everyone else does it and so and so allows their kids to do it, but that still doesn't make it alright. Even if the pastor's kids at your church are allowed to play those games or watch those movies it's still opening up a doorway for demonic powers to enter your home and your children.

There are millions of types of demons of numerous sizes, shapes and assignments, but they all have the same overall mission and that is to destroy your relationship with God, any possible way they can. They can come to you in the form of just about anything here on earth, but make no mistake about it, they are here.

In hell there was talk about how the demons were going to rob, steal and destroy your relationship with your children. They plan to do it with books, videos, games, music, teachers, and even our own government will help. Demons can do things we as humans can't do, so surround your children with prayer on a daily basis. Some of you might think this is strange, but pray over your children and plead the blood of Jesus over them, because nothing the devil has ever come up with can penetrate the blood of Jesus! Think of it like this; back when the Israelites were in Egypt and the death angel was sent to kill all of the first born, if you had lambs blood on your door posts the angel of death could not harm you. Jesus is the Lamb of God and His blood was shed for all of us and by speaking the name of Jesus, pleading the blood of Jesus over your children, you keep the demonic forces from your children. But just doing that is not all you need to do. You need to get rid of those books, CD's, videos and games, etc., or you are inviting the demons back in your house. As parents, you must do your best to keep your children away from those types of entertainment.

These things I have seen with my own eyes and have experienced firsthand. Hell is real, make no mistake about it and you are going there unless you clean up your act and ask Jesus into your life. Hell is not something to play with; there I was trapped for all eternity, never to escape. I saw so many people there that never thought they would end up in hell. These were good people, some were even former pastors of churches, deacons, Sunday school teachers, some familiar men and women from our past, very good people, but they were doomed to hell forever. I did not get to ask them how they got there; I was too worried about why I was there and how I was going to handle all this torture and where the demon was taking me.

I heard more screams and more people crying out, and I knew for sure I was going into the pit of hell and that I could never return. I just wish I could get this through to you what that felt like. It's kind of like that dream you have when you are just about asleep or just nodded off and all of a sudden you feel like you are falling. Well, it's like that, except you don't wake up and shake it off, you just keep falling and falling and falling. There is no end to it or the torture you are put through; the sounds and the smell. The smell is worse than rotted garbage and the worst sewer odor you could imagine; all combined with the smell of sulfur. I knew then with certainty I was going to just be tortured and burn in hell forever.

I was getting closer to where this demon wanted to take me; I could finally see the devil from a distance. He is not what you might picture him to be; he was actually a bright shining light and was very beautiful, but I could feel the evil that he emitted. I did not see the typically portrayed horns or a long tail, he was actually very good looking and I think that is why he is able to fool so many people. He only appears to people on earth that are very important to him, so that he can win them over. If he were gross and grotesque like the demons everyone would run from him. So many people have been fooled by him and his lies, including me. I believed the lie that marijuana was good for you because God put it on earth. Well, God may have put it on earth, but not for the purpose we are using it for. He also made cyanide, but if we use it wrong it will kill us. Some things kill the body and those things are bad but what kills your spirit is even worse.

The longer I was staying there in hell, people were grabbing ahold of me; biting me and screaming at me. Different demons were now attaching themselves to me, as well. I could feel them pulling from different directions while the one main spirit continued to hold onto my left wrist. He continually yelled at me, making fun of me and telling me that I was a loser, just like I was always told I would be. I knew now that I was lost for sure, there was no return. I was lost, and to think I had all those chances to turn things around and change my life, but my own self-satisfaction was too important to me. I thought what a fool I had been; I was truly trapped and now would have to pay the price for all eternity.

5

Arriving in Heaven

All of a sudden, I heard a voice like a mighty roar of thunder that said, "It is not his time yet. His mother has been praying for him since he was a little boy. You must release him now; I made a promise!" The evil spirit that had ahold of me released me immediately, and I seemed to just fly though space upward and out of hell in seconds. Suddenly there was bright light everywhere; everything glowed.

I felt like I had never felt before, these wonderful feelings all through my being! Not only did I now have hope, I knew I was in the presence of a heavenly being! I was just outside of this beautiful place, just outside a gate. The gate looked like it was made of pearls and it radiated in beauty, but the light that came from it and from the city inside the gate was unbelievable! It was a light that is not only seen, but that penetrates every aspect of your being. The feeling that comes over a person is so euphoric that nothing in life is sad anymore. You only feel joy and happiness; no sorrow of any kind. At this time there was nothing holding onto me like it was in hell, and I had freedom to move around so I started to go into the gate. As I moved closer, an angel appeared to me and told me I could not stay there yet; that is was not my time. I could see everything inside the gates and I could feel everything everyone else felt, but I wasn't allowed to stay or run around and do things I would have liked too.

The angel that stopped me at the gate was a massive being, much like a human but larger than life. He had hair down to his shoulders and was wearing some type of white gown that seemed to glow. His hair was sort of very light brown to a dark blonde and by earthly standards of measurement I would say he was about seven feet tall. When he spoke to me he had the gentlest voice, yet every word had such power with it. It was clear to me at that point how powerful words are, and made me instantly think about the power of God's words when He speaks. It became easy for me to understand how the whole universe was made just by His spoken word.

When we die there is an odd thing that happens. You instantly know things, everything you ever needed to know, you now know. It would be kind of like being given an entire encyclopedia and knowing everything in it in less than a second. No one has to tell you anything or describe anything to you; you just know it through your whole being. Our spirit, as I have learned, doesn't have a brain to mess things up. We get the same thinking capacity as heavenly beings have without our brains trying to analyze everything first; you just know it and accept it.

This beautiful angel went on to tell me some things about my life and what I need to do when I get back on earth. When he spoke to me, I understood everything and knew exactly what I was supposed to do when I was sent back, yet I wanted to stay. Many things he told to me or showed me I cannot discuss with you yet as I was told to keep them to myself until a time when I will be told it's okay to share it. However, there are some things I can share with you at this time.

First, I saw my father in a hospital room. The room was painted a pale yellow and my dad's bed was to the right of the room. There was an older woman there that I did not recognize as well as a few other people. My dad was lying in the bed with his eyes closed when he suddenly sat straight up pointing at me and said, "I did it to you! I did it to you!" This scared me and I asked why I had to see this and the angel spoke to me about generational curses and sin on earth, and told me when I get back to earth I will need to break that curse and sin. The generational curse is a link to your past before you were born; it goes to the third or fourth generation and sometimes even further, depending on what it is and when it began.

Another thing I can share with you is I was given several gifts; one gift is to be able to see inside a person, deep into their soul or spirit. This is not something that I turn on or off, nor can I select the person I can see into; that is up to God. This is not just reserved for church - it happens all the time at work, play, shopping or anywhere I go. I know, it sounds kind of freaky, but it was given to me for a reason and when God gives you a gift, whether it may be singing, teaching, preaching, a kind spirit, a pleasant voice… no matter what it is, use it! God gives us all different gifts and I know it hurts Him when He sees people that won't use what He gave them or uses it for the wrong purpose, but His gifts are irrevocable. What I see is the person's spirit, especially during times of worship. There are many things I see that I never say to a person, unless the Holy Spirit gives me the go ahead; that's just how it works.

I was also shown things about the future; I saw what seemed like millions of people connected to each other with these things at desks and on their laps and they were typing on them. Remember now this was in back the 70's and computers and laptops did not exist back then, or if they did, it was only a very select few that had them. There was some connection to people all over the world like a big net connecting them to each other. People could connect with other people and talk to them through these devices and see the other person on their little TV's.

Now remember, this is 1978 and many of these things seemed very strange to me. People were walking around talking to each other on phones that had no wires attached, and later with these little things stuck in the ear, and then later in time people were talking into thin air; nothing I could see was attached to them. Then it was shown to me that they had this little device that had been implanted inside their ear with a little machine and all they had to do was tap on the back or bottom of their ear and say a person's name and they could talk to that person. There was another device that looked like a small flat TV that was very thin that people walked around with talking to it and typing on it. There were many people that were all alone, walking and looking at these little phones or flat TV's, typing on them, talking into them. So many people had forgotten how to really communicate and this was all part of the devil's plan to get control of people, because if they forgot how to communicate verbally, then they would forget how to pray as well. Connect and keep them in touch with machines instead of people. I also saw buildings in space circling the earth as well as other things I will discuss as I am given permission to do so.

During this time it was also revealed to me that our nation would go through some very difficult problems, almost to the point of no return, but Christians all across the country started praying and taking action to turn it around. Some were persecuted for their stance yet it did not stop the Christians from moving forward.

There was so much that I saw as the angel spoke to me and showed me certain things, which I really had no concept of once I returned to my body. But I do know this, it all made sense to me at the time. I know that when the angel spoke of things my awareness was clear and it was easy to understand. I remember that, but once I came back into my body, my mind couldn't grasp it. Even the things in hell made sense while I was there, but when I returned to my body I had confusion about some things because I couldn't understand all of them with my brain; it just doesn't function as well as our spiritual being or mind does. It took a lot of prayer and the Holy Spirit to help make things clear.

It is impossible to express how I felt while being in heaven. It was a euphoric feeling all the time, and speaking of time, there never seemed to be time. Now I understand where it says in the Bible "a thousand years are like a day". Time really has no meaning in heaven; time is something that was made for man here on earth so he could keep records of things he did and when. God's timing is perfect and no calendar or clock can tell you when that is going to be. Yes, we have precise times and dates where the Lord said to do certain things or to show up at particular places at specified times, but that is just for us here on earth; time means nothing in heaven, there isn't day or night, it just always is.

Now I want to tell you what I saw in heaven. Most of my time was spent with this angel, but I did have time to look around some. What I noticed was that the light in heaven was everywhere; there were no shadows, no dark spots in heaven. I saw many huge homes; not like homes here in the United States, but huge structures made with pure white stone of some kind. The streets may have been gold, but the shiniest pure gold you have ever seen. There was a river flowing through heaven and the water was so clean and pure that it almost looked like noting was in the river at first. The sound of the water was like that of little children laughing and singing. Every noise I heard in heaven made me smile and filled me with joy!

There were trees in heaven, two very big, beautiful trees right next to the river running through heaven. On one tree there was one kind of fruit and on the other tree there was a different kind of fruit. Many stopped and looked up at the trees, but I did not see anyone picking fruit off of either tree. The leaves on the trees were like huge Magnolia leaves, but much bigger. They were about three or more feet long, and the branches stretched out for what seemed to be miles. Now let me explain something here; because there is no real concept of time, space, or distance in heaven and hell, I am just trying to take what I saw and put it in perspective so you can understand. When you die, all these things will become clear and explicable to you because your mind will not be there to interfere with what your spirit knows and comprehends. Our minds are only capable of what we feed it to understand, much like a computer, except that unlike a computer, we can try to reason with things and make some changes; but still only with what we already know. Let's take the sky for example; we all have been told it is blue, but if we were all told it was green, we would see it differently. In our spirit, we have the ability to understand things that are way beyond our finite minds. We can grasp things of the universe that as humans we have not yet seen nor can we see or understand until we die and are in the spirit. Many things I saw I cannot convey in words so that anyone could fully comprehend. I can't even begin to tell you what they were or even how to describe them. Our minds are limited, but our spirits are not!

I'm sure most of you have heard of the book of Revelation in the Bible. What John saw cannot be described completely in words, though he tries so hard to explain things. I am sure everything he wrote was 100% accurate, but if it was someone from today writing of those same visions, maybe it would be described differently because of things that have been invented since then. And Ezekiel, what he saw, perhaps that would be described differently today. When I saw what I now recognize as computers, tablets, and laptops, I thought there were little flat TV's with some kind of flat typewriters connected to them or tablets with an electronic typewriter inside it, and laptops were the strangest looking things to me. What I found so odd about laptops and tablets was that people had these things with them all over the place and no electricity was hooked up to many of them. People had them with them outside, by a lake, out on a boat, in the woods, all over. As I stated earlier on, I had no idea what a computer was because they didn't have home computers or laptops back then.

6

Angels, Music and More

Let me explain to you something that I learned in heaven about angels. There are different types of angels. One type of angel is much like you and me; they are about the same size as our spirits and they look like us. These angels are given different assignments to different people and they can be assigned more than one person at a time. I call them Helper angels. They are there to help you through different things in your life on earth. They can transform into looking just like you, if need be.

Next there is what I call Guardian angels. Their assignments are usually to one person at a time and they are there to actually guard you from harm. You have heard people tell stories about how they were heading into an accident that couldn't be avoided and the next thing they knew they were outside of the accident unharmed. That is because of these Guardian angels. Sometimes, though, these angels cannot perform their assignment because the person they are watching over has done something to where the angel can't do their job anymore. I will try to explain more on this later.

Angels with feathers or Winged angels; these are angels that are usually sent with a particular message to bring to a person or group of people. For example, like when Jesus was born, or many times in the Bible where angels have appeared to give someone a message from God. I'm sure most of you have heard about angels that show up at places in different churches around the world; that is usually this type of angel. There are also other very important angels that don't have wings that can also bring messages to people; it's just that the majority of messengers are Winged angels.

There are angels that their only assignment is to take answers from prayers back to you. When you pray for something there are many times these angels will be the ones to give you the answers, directly from heaven. Some of these angels have been seen, but mostly they are unseen, as they carry the message or answer to your prayer. They are very common and they are ascending and descending all the time, 24 hours around the clock. These angels can't make you accept the answers they bring back; that is determined by your will and choice.

Archangels are the biggest and most powerful angels. They usually have one assignment at a time and that assignment usually changes life as we know it here on earth. When you come into the presence of an Archangel you can feel its power, you know they represent God firsthand. The power they possess can actually change the course of time and events here on earth. If you saw an Archangel here on earth it would scare you to death. But in heaven, your spirit understands this power and that its power comes from God, not to be feared in heaven. There were very few Archangels that I saw; only three of them were visible to me.

I also saw angels whose only purpose is to worship God. They just sing praises to God and their voices are, well, angelic. I guess there is no other way to explain it; their voices combined together would make anyone hearing it feel euphoric. There were many more angels there that I did not know what their specific purpose was, but I did understand the few I have just described. There are just so many things that can be understood in the spirit which can never be put into words through the processes of one's mind because the human brain simply can't comprehend it.

The music in heaven is not like what we heard in churches back while I was growing up, or even the new contemporary music back in the 70's; it was more like chants and praises! I can tell you that songs like "Holy" that Jesus Culture group sings now is like some of the music you hear in heaven, but without the heavy electric guitar. It is total worship. The kind of music is all praise music, not like "The Old Rugged Cross" or hymn types of songs; everything is happy and praise style sounds. Think about it; you are in heaven, God and Jesus are there, and you have everything you could ever want or need, so why not praise! I think since I have been back on earth, nothing moves me more than music now, because I know the source of praise and I am constantly seeking that beautiful sound I heard while I was in heaven. You know that little girl, Jackie Evancho, who sings like an angel, well she really does sound like an angel.

Unlike here on earth where we get tired of things in a short time, in heaven the people there are so full of the Spirit of God because you are spirit and no fleshly mind to tire you out or bring you down; it's 24/7 praise and worship! Speaking bluntly, I tried a lot of different drugs back in the 70's and there wasn't anything that could give you even one, one millionth of a percent of a high like you get in heaven. Without your flesh to hold you back or to bring thoughts of sinful things into your mind, there is nothing else but praise and worship left in you. Your spirit wells up and you just start singing and praising God!

I heard music that was so soft and gentle that it would just float through your spirit as if it were a gentle breeze caressing you the whole time. Some music made you want to jump up and shout, while other times it was simply soothing and melodious to the spirit. No one in heaven sings off key; everyone has perfect pitch. Our voices go up as one when we sing there. Though we all sing different parts; bass, tenor, alto, and soprano, it all blends together as one voice. One more thing I was excited about, we do actually get to sing with the angels!

The feeling you have when you are in heaven is something that you don't ever want to go away; you never want to leave heaven. I am bringing this up again because I feel it's important to know that feelings are part of our spirit, not just our physical bodies. How many times have you heard people say, "You can't just go on feelings?" In heaven, that is not true, you can go just on feelings because your spirit doesn't have a fleshly mind like it does on earth. Your spirit hears, thinks, tastes, feels, and smells throughout your whole being, so feelings are hard to ignore once you have experienced dying and being in the spirit. Feelings in heaven are the norm, unlike here on earth where they tell you not to trust your feelings, but that is because our flesh has sin in it.

You have to understand, what we have on earth that we can see or figure out with our minds are only things of the flesh, but the spiritual world is more alive, even here, than you can see. Spirits in this world are not all from God, there are many false spirits and many very evil spirits. Most of the time you can tell when someone has the Spirit of God in them and you can tell when someone is evil, but when you die and experience it firsthand, you have a much greater awareness and knowledge of spiritual things when you come back to earth. It's kind of like the difference between someone who has never cooked before a day in their life and a chef. Now the chef is experienced and he or she knows their way around a kitchen and what foods go best with other foods, how to prepare, season and cook the food, but the person that has never cooked might know what those foods are and they may have tasted them before, but they have no idea how to fix them. The chef will know exactly which pan to use for what, how to cut the meat or vegetables a certain way, but the person that has never cooked just knows they like to eat it, not how to prepare it. What I am getting at is this, once you have experienced something, you have greater knowledge than someone who hasn't. An astronaut can tell you what it is like to experience being in space, but all we can do is imagine it or look at footage on film or video as to what it looks like, but until we go there, we really can't experience it. Sure we can go someplace and have a simulated space experience, but that's really not the same thing. I have met a couple other people who have died before and experienced heaven and they understand immediately what I mean when I say, "Our earthly minds can't understand, comprehend or conceive what our spirit knows." Therefore, trust the Spirit of God in you and don't worry about it. God knows what He is doing!

7

Deeper Experiences in Heaven

There was something else I noticed in heaven. Everyone there seemed to know each other, and when someone new came to heaven many times there would be people they had known on earth that greeted them when they arrived. This occurred most of the time, but not all of the time. Some people were met by angels and other heavenly hosts. It was exciting to see people getting greeted when they got to heaven! Watching children being met by their parents or children that had died young meeting their mother or father that died after them; that was really exciting to see! When a husband would meet his wife or wife meet her husband; what joy! No tears, just the joy that floods all of heaven. To answer the question most ask at reading this, "Does that mean you're married in heaven?" The answer is, "NO!" But you do recognize the one you were married to and happy to see them just like anyone else in your family.

There are more beings in heaven other than God, Jesus, the Holy Spirit, us and the angels. There are other heavenly beings that I find it difficult to describe, and others that I will attempt to give my best description. There are beings that walk around heaven just praising the Lord. They look like nothing we have on earth to compare them with, but they are beautiful and sing with power and authority. They go around heaven making sure that praises of God are being lifted up in every section of heaven. They are human like with big beautiful eyes, and they have small chubby legs and arms; kind of like a chubby little baby with a rather big mouth. They just seem to float around in heaven as they sing.

There was one being that I could not get close enough to, which makes it difficult for me to describe it very well to you, but it had many eyes on it, in fact, thousands of eyes or more all over its body and wings. I could see the eyes going back and forth as if looking for something or someone, and although at the time I understood clearly the purpose, now I am unsure as to what that was. This being was much further in towards the middle of heaven.

Towards what I would call the center of heaven was this very bright light, brighter than our sun but it did not hurt me to look at it; it was kind of like looking at lightning so pure and white. The feeling I got when I gazed at that light was so pure and overwhelming with nothing but love; a love like I had never before experienced. I felt like I was being drawn to it, like it just pulled at everything inside me to go to it, but I was not allowed to go that far because I had not done what I needed to do on earth to be allowed up there to stay. I wish I could somehow convey the feeling that came over me; it was so powerful and soothing at the same time. I knew that I was in the presence of the Holy of Holies in heaven.

I can remember the sounds, smells and feelings of heaven as I walked around there; it's something I will never forget as long as I live. I recall the laughter, singing, praises, and beautifulness of everything and everybody.

If you are reading this and you are not a Christian I strongly suggest you make a change in your life here on earth, because this is just a snap of the fingers long and your afterlife is forever. I am not talking about just as long as a hundred years, but for all eternity; forever and ever. That's longer than it would take you to walk around the world a million times, in fact, that would be less than a second in heaven. Get my point? It is real. Heaven and hell are the final destinations and my question is which one do you want to be in forever? I'm not trying to get religious on you; I'm trying to save your life. Think about it while you finish reading this book.

There were some other things I was shown in heaven about the future of our earth. There were people on earth that were there strictly to corrupt the world, the leaders and the common people. These people were possessed of a spirit that leads people into false hopes and delusions. Many people on earth believed these leaders as they convinced the people of earth that everything would be good for them if they just trusted them.

Homosexuality was coming to a peak in the future where it seemed the majority of people were accepting it and the ones that didn't were actually being persecuted and prosecuted in many parts of the world. This angered God!

The other spirit that was entering into people caused them to lust after children and parents gave their children away to others who said they loved their children. Some parents even sold their children to these evil and vile people. Not only were men seeking these children, but women, too. Some wanted to perform homosexual acts on these children and other heterosexual sexual acts on them. This was being accepted in many parts of the world, and it greatly angered God, too!

There was another spirit of lust that was prevalent in the world and that was a lust for power and control. This lust came out of the Middle East and was spreading around the world at an alarming rate. It was disguised as a form of religion and relied heavily on recruiting young people believing in the lies they were told of wonderful places and experiences they would have if they just obeyed. It was the ultimate mind control of our youth. An army was being raised to take over the world one place at a time, but wearing down all the earth as much as possible. Many of these were little children, from the time of their birth, they were told that Christians were the enemy. Some of these children attended schools that taught them not to love anyone that was not of their faith, but to hate them. However, this spirit of lust for control and power will never be successful because the Spirit of God will not allow it, and the people of this earth will eventually revolt.

I saw Israel standing alone; many nations had separated themselves from Israel, yet Israel had done nothing wrong to deserve it. Even the United States was taking action that harmed Israel. I saw many European nations take a stand against Israel as well, but all these European nations and the United States finally turned things around, but only after some damage was already done. These nations changed their minds after they realized they had been lied to and used. I saw lies, lies and more lies, coming out of the Middle East. Israel was the only nation telling the truth!

Many of the things I saw then, in my visit to heaven, have now come to pass and has angered God. The people of the earth need a wakeup call, and that is coming soon. There will be great storms, earthquakes, and many more natural disasters that will occur not just in the United States, but in the entire world. Remember, these things were revealed to me back in 1978 before the big 9.0 earthquake struck Japan, and the tsunamis, and the worst typhoon in recorded history that hit the Philippine Islands. I can tell you that these events are just the beginning, but those who are solid in the Lord and really do put Him first will be warned. The angel showed me that there are a few people on earth right now that know about these things and that they are the intercessors praying for our country. These are not necessarily the big evangelists or TV preachers, but regular individuals who are the intercessors on their face before the Lord daily. Now, there are going to be some major preachers that are going to finally stand up against this filth and immorality, but that time is still to come. I was not to know the exact times when these things would happen, but I am certainly aware that it has started.

Another thing that was shown to me was the spirit of deception within the church; accompanied by the spirit of self-righteousness. There were people of all religions belonging to churches that were going around trying to divide up the church in order to satisfy their own righteousness. They would go to other individuals in the church and spread lies and rumors about certain ministers in the church; attacking the pastors and worship leaders. These rumors would spread like wildfire, even those that knew better would start believing because the spirit of deception was so strong and the people of the church were not prayed up enough to know the difference. Satan is well aware that if he can divide the church, he can conquer it, too, and steal away people from the church. However, this, too, will come to a stop by the power of the Holy Spirit. The people trying to do this will be exposed and they will be accountable for the ones they led astray, unless they repent.

Something else the angel talked to me about was 'Hidden Intentional Sins' (HIS). These are sins that people who claim to be Christians do frequently on a regular basis. Let me explain; if you are a Christian, you know right from wrong from the Holy Spirit indwelling within you. But if you think that right and wrong are only what other people see in you, you are deceiving yourself. What has been happening is that many people are claiming one thing and behind closed doors are doing another. If you are looking at porn, treating your family badly, cheating on your spouse, are into violent or graphic gaming, using illegal drugs or abusing prescription drugs, or drinking alcoholic beverages daily, and you are hiding these things, then that is your hidden intentional sin. These are not the only ones, there are many more, like aggravating your children, lusting after your fellow coworker, cussing, anything that you would not do in front of Jesus if He were standing next to you. Doing these things over and over again when you know it is wrong; that is intentional sinning.

Hidden Intentional Sinning (HIS) has become one of the worst epidemics in the Christian community; it surpasses anything close to it by a mile. The angel said that this displeases God greatly and He wants it made known. He said that if people do not repent, then He will expose them, from the top evangelist on down to the quietest person at church. I want to further elaborate that I am not talking about sin that is unintentional, I am talking about sin that you know is wrong, yet you intentionally choose to repeat the behavior. You are not fooling anyone but yourself. Believe it or not, many times people know that you are doing it, but they don't say anything because they don't want to embarrass you. Don't you think you are going to hate it when it is exposed to everyone and they all find out what you are doing? I mean, what if you are beating your spouse, looking at porn or lusting after someone while you are married, do you really want that exposed? Do you?

For me, it's a little different; I have been charged with warning you because I have been there and you don't want to go to hell! I am being sent with this warning, either you repent and change your ways, or it will be exposed. The time for you to take heed in what I am saying is now; you have been warned by reading this book.

Let me ask you a question, if you see a three year old child walking along the side of the road and they turn to walk directly into oncoming traffic going 75 mph, what would you do? Would you just keep driving away looking in the other direction and hope someone else will stop and help them, or think maybe they will magically make it through to the other side? I would be willing to bet most of you would you come to a screeching halt, jump out of your car and rescue them. That is what I am doing by warning you about this. This is the most stoppable sin there is, because you already know it's wrong and you know the right way to go, so please stop before it's too late! You have no idea how many people I saw in hell that didn't belong there. Well, they didn't think they did, but hidden intentional sin has been rampant for many years now and getting worse every day; especially with all the new technology continually coming out. In the near future this technology will even produce human like forms that will be part of the worst lust the word has ever seen.

8

Back to Earth

So many things we don't know here on earth will all be revealed to us when we get to heaven and you will know it all as soon as you get there. I can tell you this; there is no sorrow, no pain and no regrets in heaven. I wish I could explain everything as I saw it and felt it, but it is beyond what the human mind can comprehend. When you get to heaven you will not be worrying about your children or other loved ones here on earth because you will be in the presence of God and that is something that just can't be explained.

I do want to tell you more about why I was spared from hell and it has nothing to do with me or my cries for help while in hell. The angel that spoke to me in heaven told me that God was honoring my mother's prayers because she has been so faithful to God in her life and that over 20,000 prayers have been said by her for me and God made her a promise about her children. She prayed for me two to three times daily. Can you imagine 20,000 times that you've been prayed for? My mother is a Godly woman and brought all of her children up in the ways of the Lord and in church. The paths we took may not have been right, but she knew that if she raised us in the ways of the Lord, we would all return someday if we drifted away. Mom, you were right about that one!

This heavenly being, the angel, explained to me that everyone that goes to hell cries out for God but that it is too late for them. I was just one out of maybe five-hundred billion that ever escape hell and it wasn't because of anything I did on earth or how I lived, but because of my mother's prayers. Parents, never stop praying for your children. Even when it looks impossible, keep praying for them and never give up.

When the angel was finished telling me things, it allowed me to stand just inside the gate and view what heaven was like for some time. Oh, I did not want to leave, I didn't want to go back to earth; this was so beautiful and wonderful. The music that you hear literally goes though you, you feel the music and the singing; it pierces every part of your being and it is so beautiful and uplifting! I thought, "Please God, I don't want to go back to earth", but I could not stay there because I had to change my life in order to get back to heaven and I had a job to do; write this book.

The final thing the angel told me was, "You must wait to tell about your experience until you are told to do so." I understood that this was a warning and I also knew that my life was not where it was supposed to be and that I needed to turn things around.

Back to earth I went and in a blink of an eye, I was entering my bedroom. There in the room were the two paramedics that had just arrived. One paramedic was feeling my neck for a pulse and he shook his head looking back over his right shoulder to the other paramedic standing behind him. The man behind him was getting something out of a medical bag while the one that checked my pulse was getting ready to turn me onto my back, as I was lying on my left side facing towards a wall. Just then my spirit moved into my body and started to wake it up. It shook my body violently, vibrating like I had just been hit with electricity, and it actually scared the paramedics. All of a sudden, I was able to breathe and I opened my eyes and stared straight at this surprised paramedic. I will never forget the look on his face as he asked, "Are you alright?" in a startled voice. I replied that I was, though I was sort of in some kind of shock because I was back in my body here on earth. They insisted on checking me thoroughly and after about twenty minutes or so they could not find anything wrong with me and they left. First though, they tried to get me to go with them to the hospital, but I refused to go. I was aware that something significant had occurred and I was trying my best to sort it all out, but wasn't afraid to stay at home; I knew nothing else would happen to me. By the way, I did say a quick short prayer, "Lord forgive me of my sins, I accept Jesus as my Lord and Savior. Amen!"

I could not sleep the rest of that night; I didn't want to smoke anymore pot or do anything except sit there and wonder about what just happened to me. The paramedics had told me that my girlfriend called around 11:45 p.m. and they got there in about five minutes. My body was cool to the touch and blue. I had no pulse and wasn't breathing; I was dead. They also told me that they had never seen anyone do what I did when I came back to life, vibrating like I did, it startled them. I know that I was trying to wake my body up, shake it, whatever I had to do because it was so stiff and I couldn't breathe.

The next morning about 6:00 a.m., I got up and went to the hospital to see the doctor that had been treating me for the blood clot. I arrived there around 6:30 a.m., no traffic at all at that time in the morning in Grand Rapids, Michigan. The doctor had an office that he used for consultations at the hospital and I sat on the floor waiting till he came in so I could talk to him. A little after 7:00 o'clock the doctor arrived, and I asked him if I could please talk to him before he started his rounds. He agreed, and when we went into his office I started to tell him what happened to me. You have to understand I was scared to death thinking I was going nuts or something. I talked for over an hour as the doctor listened to me with such interest, then I asked him, "Am I nuts or did this really happen to me?" I can remember the doctor clearly telling me, "What happened to you, I believe was real. I am not saying that you just think it is real, I am saying it really happened." He went on to tell me that he'd had a couple patients that had died and came back to life and they told him things similar to what I told him, except they had not gone to hell. I was the first to tell him about hell. He also explained that the clot was so big that he had worried when the blood was thinned out that some of the clot would move into my heart or my lungs and that is why they kept me there for two weeks like they had done instead of one week.

9

Now What Do I Do?

"Now what do I do?" I wondered. I had died, gone to hell and then to heaven. I thought, "Who is ever going to believe this?" I was very confused, but I kept remembering what the angel had told me just before coming back to earth, "You must wait to tell about your experience until you are told to do so." I had no idea when that was going to be. I was hoping that by 1980 I would be ready, but I was far from it then. It wasn't until 1994 that I turned my life completely around to the Lord. Now don't get me wrong, I had stopped drinking and doing drugs, and I had quit sleeping around with so many women and a lot of other sinful things before 1994, but it wasn't until August of 1994 when I finally made a 100% commitment to God.

In July of 1994 I moved my family from Nashville, Tennessee to Albuquerque, New Mexico. I was married and we had a child; a boy named Christopher who had been born in 1985. I taught Christopher how to pray, to ask the blessing over the food, and I taught him about Jesus. But I hadn't taken him to church. I remember that August of 1994, a new neighbor named Dana came over and introduced herself to us and invited us to attend her church. I knew it was time to start doing that; going to church. Christopher was eight at the time, about to turn nine in December. He needed to know more about the Lord and I knew it was the right thing to do; especially because he needed kids his age so they could learn things about the Lord together.

So that August - after just moving to Albuquerque, Dana and her husband, Nick, invited us over to dinner and to play Bible Pictionary. Well, I had been raised in church, and had actually been in heaven, so I thought I would do real well at this game. As it turned out, it was the Bible Pictionary game for children that we played, and I did horrible. Talk about being shocked, everyone else knew the answers and I didn't remember them until after they were answered by someone else. I felt like a fool. That night I decided I was never going to be that bad at this game again so I decided to start reading the Bible.

The very next morning I got up early, opened my Bible and started reading from Genesis chapter one, verse one. That's right; I had decided that I was going to read it from cover to cover. I was told that if I just read three chapters of the Bible each day that I would be able to read the whole Bible in one year. I thought, "Hey, I can do that." So I read all three chapters that morning and every morning for a whole year; well almost. There were times, like when I got to Psalms 119, that I only read that one chapter, but other days I read four or five to make up for it.

Now a year was over and I can still remember when I finished reading that last verse in Revelation, chapter 22, verse 21, "The grace of the Lord Jesus be with God's people. Amen." Whoopee! I had just finished reading the whole Bible! I can remember thinking to myself, "Wow, Ivan, how many other people have actually read every word in the Bible from cover to cover?" I was so proud of this accomplishment! Then it was like a voice I could hear say, "Now what?" I thought, "Now what, I read the whole Bible. That's what's now what." Then I heard that voice again, "So what all do you remember?" I answered, "Well, I remember about Adam and Eve, and Noah, and Moses, and Job, and about Jesus, and other things." And the voice said, "What can you quote?" Well, that didn't go over well with me because the only scripture I could quote was John 3:16, "For God so loved the world that He gave His only begotten son that whosoever believes in Him shall not perish but have eternal life." - So I knew I needed more work on that part, and then I heard the voice again. "Read it again." Read it again? But I just finished it. "Read it again", the voice said one more time. Okay, I got the message and started all over again to read it and have been doing that just about every year since 1994.

Here's something I learned about reading the Bible; there is something new in it every day no matter how many times you read it. My Bible is so worn down, marked up and falling apart, but it is still my Bible and I discover new meaning in it every single day! I knew one day that I would like to pass this old marked up, torn up Bible to my son, Christopher, and that day was this past Christmas.

It is clear that I had to mature; not just as a person, but spiritually as well. I used to wonder why the Lord was not allowing me to write this book about what I went through, but it has become very clear to me that I needed to be rooted in the Word and my prayer life more. I have made a lot of mistakes since 1978 and wondered why I made all those mistakes when I knew better. I guess it just goes to show that human nature needs to be kept in check at all times, and I was not doing that very well for a while.

Over the last four years I have spent many days and nights on my face before the Lord, and I have been studying the Word of God more. My walk with the Lord is so strong now, especially after the Lord removed some things out of my life to clear the way for me to write this book. This past year beginning in January, 2013, I started attending Skyway Church in Goodyear, Arizona, and they have an open prayer service every Wednesday morning that I try attend every week. This prayer service is something that churches need today because it is giving the church insight and a unity in serving the Lord. It seems there were only about thirty or so that attended back in March and now in late 2013, there are about one hundred or so - it's catching on. This is a great place to get corporate prayer going for certain things and it also allows you to celebrate God in prayer and praise with others; which gives me strength!

I mention this because many churches today are so concerned about the show they put on and not as concerned about what the people attending need, and if all you get is a twenty minute sermon and three to five songs every week, how is that really helping your people? We need to seek the face of God.

Back when I was a kid at Evangel Assembly of God church in Forestville, Maryland, we used to have real prayer services where we really sought out after the Lord. Sometimes we would start out praying at 7:00 p.m. in the evening and not finish until midnight. Every New Year's Eve we would gather at church around 9:00 p.m. for some songs and a few words from our pastor and then we would get on our knees and pray in the New Year and not leave until 1:00 or 2:00 in the morning. Today most churches that have a New Year's Eve service, it is a quick service and off you go; they start to flicker the lights fifteen minutes after midnight to let you know it's time to leave. I am not saying we need to be like we used to be, but we do need to get serious about the Lord.

There are new moves of the Spirit of the Lord and the old ways do not fit in the new ways, like the new wine does not fit into the old wineskins. We have to adapt, but we should never lose sight of worship and spending time in prayer. Think about this; how many times in the New Testament do you read about Jesus praying? I mean after all, He is the son of God; did he really need to pray? Well, if Jesus needed it, then so do we! We need it a lot more than Jesus did and we seem to think that all we need to do is say a little prayer every night and ask the blessing before or after each meal and we are good to go; but I am telling you that is not enough. Jesus is coming back for a church that is ready for Him, not a group of people that are lukewarm.

What I am getting at is this, I know I have been to hell and heaven and I know I need a lot more of God in my life; I cannot disappoint Him anymore. Many of you reading this book know that you need to turn up the fire in your life, too. Quit playing church or playing games. Search your heart and make a decision to turn up the heat in your own life. It doesn't matter what church you go to, but it does matter what you are being taught and how much time you put into the Lord. The church is not going to save you or get you to heaven; that is up to you ONLY!

The old style of pastors doing everything at the church is changing and it needs to change. We are the church, not that building you walk into every Sunday. We need to all be more active in what we do. It is not up to the pastor of the church to minister to everyone; that is our job as

Christians but you can't do it if you aren't prayed up and read up.

What I am getting at is that there is a new move of the Holy Spirit that is beginning to spread throughout the world, and if you just go to church on Sunday and maybe Wednesday night services and you aren't exploring more on your own about the move of the Spirit, you are going to miss it. In fact, you will be one of those people that will be sitting on the sidelines judging it. Too many people in the past and in the coming future are willing to criticize the move of the Spirit; like they know it all and they know everything that God can do, and God hasn't checked with them yet to get their approval. I've got news for you; God doesn't need your approval. He's going to do it anyways! Remember, Jesus said to do these things and greater, so how do you get to greater? By reading His Word and spending time in prayer.

Sometimes when I am talking about the Lord and what He's done for me and sharing things I have to say, I have had people ask me, "Who gave you the authority to say that?" I love the look on their faces when I tell them, "Jesus!" They get all bent out of shape and twisted up and then they can't help but say, "So are you telling me Jesus talks directly to you?" "Why yes, He does, and He talks to you, too. In fact, I think He asked your permission yesterday if it was okay to talk to me." That is my reply, and that usually ends that. They have no idea how to answer me after I say that to them, some get huffy and walk away and others just stare at me trying to come up with an answer, but they never do.

What I am trying to get to here is that we all serve the same God and God is not into religion, He is into having a relationship with you. Adam didn't have any religion, yet he talked with God in the garden. Moses didn't have a religion, yet he spoke directly to God and God used him to deliver His people out of Egypt. It's not religion that is going to get you to heaven; it is your personal walk with the Lord. Here is something simple to do, ask God to allow the Holy Spirit to be your teacher when you read the Bible, that's what I did and the Holy Spirit was my teacher. My eyes were opened and things were revealed to me and still are every day!

Another thing, quit laying the blame on everyone else for you not being where you are supposed to be with the Lord. It is not their fault, it is yours. Stop blaming that pastor at the church you used to go to; you know, that one that hurt your feelings because he didn't do something the way you wanted him to do it, or he said something that offended you. You keep hanging on to that lie and you will be going straight to hell when you die. I promise you, there are a lot of people in hell that fell for this lie, just like you.

Hell is not a figment of imagination and it's not just for really bad people; it is also for those who have turned their back on the Lord. I ought to know; I've been there and done that. Why are you going to let other people affect your walk with the Lord? You can't afford it and you don't have time enough in life, either. I was only 26 years old when I died, and I am one of the very rare lucky ones that got to come back and straighten out my life. Hell is for real! Don't keep playing around or you are going to be one of those people that everyone is going to go to your funeral and say, "I sure hope he made it."

I am not God. I can't tell you whether you are going to hell or not, that is solely up to God. But I can tell you these things I have been shown and told so that you can escape hell. I can't tell you if you are going to heaven or not either, but you can decide that yourself by giving your heart to the Lord, accepting Jesus as your Lord and Savior, and then living the life you are supposed to live. Don't believe the lie that you can live like hell after you give your heart to the Lord and still get to heaven. I am living proof that that doesn't work, and thank God I am living proof because the other people who have done that and died are still in hell; forever. I still get queasy when I think about it, lost in eternity forever and ever and ever...

Something I didn't find out until this past Spring of 2013, was that during that time in my life when I was not living for the Lord, back in 1978, my grandmother had a vision or dream about me. She told my mother and everyone else back then that she saw me standing on a huge rock and I was preaching and singing. My mother never told me about it because she thought my grandmother was crazy. I mean, after all, I was not living for the Lord at that time and my mother knew I was into drugs. At that time, and for many years, I did not live near my mother or grandmother nor did I ever get a chance to talk to my grandmother on the phone; she lived in the mountains in Maryland and I lived in Michigan at the time. My mother also lived in Maryland and though we did talk on the phone occasionally, my mother knew I was not living for the Lord and that I was into drugs, so she decided not to tell me at the time and just forgot after a while. In the Spring of 2013, while talking to my mother on the phone about being an ordained minister, my mother remembered what my grandmother told her and explained how excited my grandmother was and how she was telling everyone in great detail about my preaching and singing. I wonder what she knew and exactly what day she had that dream or vision. My grandmother passed away March 26, 2003; before I could ask her about it. She was 94 when she passed.

Here is something else to really think about; I have had ADHD all my life and if you know anything about anyone with ADHD, you know they can't keep track of something for more than a few seconds, but us adult ADHD can actually pay attention for up to two minutes! Can you believe that God has blessed me enough to allow me to sit down and write this book? I'm great at writing TV commercials, they are all but thirty seconds or sixty seconds long, but for me this book is like writing a whole movie! There are days when I have sat for six to eight hours straight just typing away. That is unheard of for people like me, but we can do mighty things when God calls us to do it!

10

My Father

Let me explain to you the relationship between my father and me. My father was born in Hannibal, Missouri, back in 1926 and he was raised on a farm until he was about ten, then they moved to San Pedro, California until he was about twelve, and then his family moved to Washington, D.C. He had a brother, but he got killed in World War II, and he had a sister, too, but she died in her early forties from the same heart disease that eventually took my father. My whole family on my dad's side has something called Cardiomyopathy. Each of my blood sisters and my only brother have it, their children have it, and so do all of their grandchildren. My son and I do not have it, nor will we ever get it. This has to do with the generational sin and curses I was told to break by the angel in heaven.

My heart was checked around 1974 and they said I had some abnormalities in it. I was told I had a larger left side to my heart than normal, which is a form of Cardiomyopathy. I never had any heart attacks or anything, just some pressure once in a while. I had not had a Doppler echo done to my heart back then, am not sure if they even had it then, but the doctors told me I have this problem. But since I went to heaven and came back and broke the generational curse, I am free of any hint of it.

I'm sure some of you think this is really an odd thing that God can break not only the generational sin, but also physical curses that are in your family tree linked to you. This type of Cardiomyopathy is a generational curse; it came from my father's maternal side of the family. My grandmother on my father's side died when I was only about a year old from this disease, too. It has been passed down from one generation to the next for at least four or five generations that we were able to discover, and now it has spread to three more generations.

If you remember, when I was in heaven I saw my father sit up in his hospital bed and he said, "I did it to you. I did it to you." This was part of what he was talking about; he passed on that physical curse of Cardiomyopathy down through his children. Because I was made aware of what it was and where it came from, I was able through prayer and fasting to break that curse in Jesus name, and it no longer has power over me. My heart and my blood no longer have any signs of this incurable disease. My oldest sister, Carolyn, had bad problems with it, though. She got a heart transplant from the Cleveland Clinic back in either 2001 or 2002, but she only lived one more year. However, she did not die of a heart problem, but from a brain tumor. She was only 56. Carolyn started the first

Cardiomyopathy Association in the world over in England. She was very successful in teaching not only common people about this condition, but she also taught doctors about it; she was very educated and extremely smart. You can look up Carolyn Biro and the Cardiomyopathy Association in the United Kingdom on the web at http://www.cardiomyopathy.org/Carolyn-Biro.html.

My sisters, my brother, and I had our blood tested for a genetic study to see if they could find the marker in our blood back in 1990. I did not have it but everyone else did and that is because the curse was broken. Unfortunately, my older sister, Kathy, suffers from the disease now. Kathy's daughter had open heart surgery when she was in her late twenties to help her heart pump blood properly. The surgery was successful for her; she is in her forties at the writing of this book. Now that you understand this part, let me talk more about my relationship with my father.

In December of 1981 my father and I finally had a healing moment. My father and I both lived in Lakeland, Florida, at the time and my dad had divorced my mother about two years before and eventually married another woman; her name was Margret. I called my father up on the phone in early December and asked him if I could come over to visit. He said, "Sure, come on over. Margret is at work and I'm just watching TV." So I went over to his house; this was around 10:30 or so in the morning. I knocked on his door and he yelled "Come on in, it's unlocked." I went inside and said hi to my dad; he was sitting in his easy chair watching some game show on TV. I walk over to the breakfast bar across the room from the front door and sat on a stool. My father asked me, "What are you doing today?" I said, "I just wanted to come over and talk with you dad." "What about," he asked.

I decided it was time I found out what made my dad so angry when I was a child. "Dad," I said, sounding as if I was going to ask a question. My father said, "What?" "Dad, I would like to ask for you to forgive me for whatever it was that I did to you as a kid that got you so upset to have to beat me like you did." You could hear a pin drop; not one sound and no movement from my dad. I thought for sure he was going to blow up at me, and then I saw something I had never seen before; my father was crying. These were not little tears, they were coming out in buckets and even to the point the front of his shirt was getting soaked. Then he stood up and turned to me and said, "No, forgive me," as he put his arms out to hug me. Needless to say, I started crying, too. My father had never hugged me in his life, nor had he ever apologized about anything, and here he was hugging me and saying he was sorry.

This was the first time in my father's life I had ever seen him actually cry, and those tears were for me. He had only shed one tear when I saw him when his father died, but other than that one tear - he'd never cried in front of me, and now he was crying for how he treated me. Thank you God!

My father then proceeded to tell me why he mistreated me as a child and he truly wanted forgiveness because he knew it was wrong. My father repented to me that day, and from that day forward he told me things he had never told anyone before; he wanted to set the record straight. For the next five months my father and I had a close relationship where we saw each other several times a week and chatted on the phone a lot, too.

Then April 1, 1982 came around and my father had another heart attack. This was maybe his seventh or eighth one, I can't really remember, but his heart was so bad it didn't matter. My dad was going into the hospital and he called me and asked me to meet him there. I left work and went straight there. I can remember him being excited when he saw me, he said he had something to say to me and wanted to do it in private. Finally, the doctors and nurses left the room and my father told me, "Son, I am going to leave here next Wednesday, one way or another. Either they are going to find a way to fix my heart or I am just going to leave this earth." That was a shocker for me to hear my father say that, as he had always been such a positive person about his condition. At this point his heart was so enlarged it could hardly beat, and my father had been used to always being a very active man.

During his weeks stay I visited him several times and he told me more things he said he had never told anyone before. That Tuesday night I called him on the phone and he said, "Tomorrow's the day, one way or another." He still seemed too full of life to be dying so I never thought much about what he said. Around 6:45 the next morning, Wednesday, April 7th, I got a call from the hospital. They told me that my dad was in a coma and I'd better rush down there. I got to the hospital around 7:30 a.m. or so, and his new wife and her daughter were there, as well as some other lady that was there, too. I felt like I was in the room with a bunch of strangers; wondering what they were doing in there when my father was dying.

I walked around the bed to his right side and held his hand and let him know I was there. I spoke to him, but there was no response. Then a nurse walked in to monitor my dad's vital signs; check his pulse, etc. When she lifted up one of his eyelids I could see his eyes were rolled back. I went out in the hallway and called a preacher friend of mine, Pastor Wayne Friedt, and he came up to the hospital around 9:00 that morning. While I was waiting for Wayne to arrive, I recalled I had seen this same hospital room and my dad in that exact same bed before, when I was in heaven. Now Pastor Wayne arrived, walked into the room, looked at my dad and then asked me if I would come out in the hall with him.

I followed Pastor Wayne out into the hallway and he said, "I don't think I am supposed to pray for your father's healing. I believe I am supposed to do a sinner's prayer with him." I was kind of hurt at first because I saw so many people that were very ill get healed when Pastor Wayne prayed for them, but I also knew he was led by the Spirit as to what to do, so I agreed. But I told Pastor Wayne, "My dad is in a coma, how are you going to do a sinners prayer for him when he doesn't even know you are there?" Pastor Wayne said, "Don't worry about it, God will work something out." With that, we walked back into the room.

Pastor Wayne went over to my dad's right side and took ahold of my father's hand like you would in a hand shake and said, "Mr. Tuttle, I'm Pastor Wayne Friedt and I am going to say a prayer with you." Now I can remember this as clear as if it happened ten seconds ago. My father opened his eyes slightly, barely tilted his head up, and said, "I've been waiting for you." With that, Pastor Wayne said a prayer, my dad mumbled it after him and after Pastor Wayne said, "Amen", my father went right back into his coma. Pastor Wayne left right after that and my dad passed away within seconds.

Praise God my father was able to say this prayer before he died. It's not the way it should be done so close to death, but I had witnessed my father's salvation years before when I spent that short time in heaven. Although at that time I didn't understand why everything happened like it did when I came back into my body, I now know when it is my time to go to heaven that I will be greeted by my father!

When I do get in heaven (and I know I am going there this time to stay) I now have my father and my oldest sister that I will see again!

11

Final Words

If you have read this book this far then I think it's only fair I explain a few more things to you. I am a Spirit filled Christian; I believe in all the gifts of the Spirit. I believe that people can get healed by the power of God, that the lame can walk and the blind can see, that demonic powers can be cast out or off of a person, and I believe in the full gospel of Jesus Christ. I believe in miracles, and yes, they happen today. I also believe that we have not even begun to scratch the surface of what God is going to release here on earth, and that the Great Outpouring of the Holy Spirit has not yet appeared in its fullness, that is still to come.

I know for a fact that there are things that will be coming, that have not happened yet, and that are going to be greater than anything that has ever been seen on earth. I also know that 2014 will be the year when some special gifts and an extraordinary outpouring will begin here on earth. There will be signs in the heavens and on earth, these are but warnings that you must repent, turn away from your old ways and seek the face of God. Then in the year 2016, beginning in August, there will be another type of Spiritual Gift that will be poured out among His people. These two years hold great significance in things to come.

There will be manifestations in the Spirit that have never been shown to man before, but be aware of false prophets. The false prophets will be known by their greed, not just for money, but their greed to have everyone believe and follow them. Be smart; stay in the Bible, pray daily to God, be filled with the Holy Spirit, and read His Word and seek Him daily. Reading the Bible daily does not get you to heaven, accepting Jesus as your Lord and Savior does that, but reading His Word gives you strength and allows your spirit to grow in the ways of the Lord and it will give you wisdom; Godly wisdom.

As I explained in earlier chapters, our minds can't fathom what the spirit can and being prayed up and having the knowledge God gave us to study in His Word, gives us good judgment and understanding. There is much more than the few words I have written in this book for you to read. You can have a real, personal relationship with Jesus and there are many more things in store for you if you will just seek Him and ask Him. Read God's Word and you will soon understand that there is much more for you than just reading His Word and praying, but that is where it starts.

I am not pushing any religion on you, I am just trying to help you perceive that there is more to life and death than what we can know with our minds, and that God loves everyone. He sent His Son to die for us so that we might be able to go to heaven. What I am attempting to do is help you so you can look in your Bible and see that what I am talking about is already there in your Bible. Look in the book of Acts. In the world today, with all the demonic activity, you need everything heaven can give you. So take advantage of it while you can, because after you die it is too late.

This is the time where we will all start seeing the Spirit of the Lord sweep across the earth. It's not going to be limited to here in the U.S.; it is going to move through China, India, Europe, Canada, England, Australia, New Zealand, South America, Japan, Thailand, all of Asia, Mexico, Africa, and all around the entire globe. China will experience one of the biggest explosions of the Holy Spirit, even some of those in the government are going to accept Jesus and receive the Holy Spirit! There are going to be small villages in China that have been pretty much unheard of before, and everyone in those villages will be saved and filled with the Holy Spirit. Even people in Tibet will be filled with the Spirit! This phenomenon is going to start happening in August of 2014.

While I was in heaven, I was given these dates and others and was told not to release anything till I was given the okay by the Spirit. I have kept all this information and more since 1978. I didn't have any idea what I was going to grow up to be like, or what life was even going to be like when I got older, but I had to keep quiet until now. Part of the reason for that is because the world would not have been ready for it before; there had to be a couple different moves by the Holy Spirit before people would understand these things, and even so, there are still going to be those who don't believe; but that is their chance they take.

The Spirit of the Lord is going to be poured out over the world like never before; there are going to be things happening that will shake up many churches. Some churches are going to come up against this move of the Spirit, some churches will embrace it. Most importantly, there are going to be people that have no real church association that are going to not only accept it, but move in it as well. This great outpouring of the Holy Spirit is not going to be limited to the churches. There will be people all over the world that have never heard about the Holy Spirit before, get saved and filled with the Holy Spirit, and immediately they will start performing miracles through the power of the Holy Spirit. They will lay hands on the sick and they will recover, they will cast out demonic spirits in Jesus name because the Spirit has given them power to do these things.

There are going to be people that aren't Christians at all that will be sitting in their own home watching TV or on their computer and the convicting power of the Holy Spirit will fall on them. They will give their hearts to the Lord, accept Jesus in their hearts and be filled with the Holy Spirit even though they know nothing about Jesus or the Holy Spirit, except someone mentioned Jesus before to them. Again, this is not limited to the United States, this will be happening globally in every nation around the world. The Holy Spirit will be moving upon these people to convict them of their sins. It will not come from hearing a preacher or even someone witnessing to them, it will just be part of the Great Outpouring of the Holy Spirit!

When you understand things of a spiritual nature then the things I am talking about will make perfect sense to you. There are many more things that were revealed to me and sometime soon I will be writing more about them, but in the meantime, take heed what the Spirit of God has revealed. Those of you with HIS (Hidden Intentional Sin) need to get on your face before the Lord and repent; which means to not only ask for forgiveness, but it means to change your ways. The warning about HIS is a very stern warning and it has been given in order to save your life, not to embarrass you nor condemn you. God does not want your sin to be revealed to everyone. He just wants you to repent, in private if necessary, and change your lifestyle. God loves you!

I am not perfect, I have done things in my life I am ashamed of, I have sinned, and I have had Hidden

Intentional Sin in my life. I broke the law years ago and I am totally unworthy to write this book except that I have been forgiven, cleansed, and sanctified through the blood of Jesus. I am a servant of Christ and only justified through Christ to be an authority on what I have been through. If it wasn't for my mother praying for me all these years, I wouldn't be here today to write this book; it would have been a much worse ending. Thank you mother, thank you so much!

"I pray that since you have read these things in this book that if you need help with repentance, that the Holy Spirit will help you. I pray that each and every one of you that has not accepted God as your personal Savior will accept Him now and have the understanding that Jesus died on the cross to forgive you of your sins. I also pray that you seek more about the Lord and the Holy Spirit as you finish reading this book, too, but most of all, that you give your life to Jesus. All these things are gifts from God to anyone who asks, so I pray that you do ask God to do these things, for you today." Now would be a good time in your life to get another book which is much better than this one, it's called the Bible and start reading it every day.

"If You Want to Make Sure You're Going to Heaven"

Here is a simple prayer you can say out loud right now, if you have not accepted Jesus into your heart. "Lord Jesus, I come before you today asking that you forgive me of my sins. I accept you, Jesus, into my heart. I know you died on the cross to forgive me of my sins and you rose from the grave and are seated at the right hand of your Father. I repent of my sins, I will turn away from the things I have been doing wrong. I thank you, Lord, for coming into my heart now. I know now that your Spirit dwells in me. I make you Lord and Savior over my life. In Jesus name I pray. Amen." It's that simple; now you are a child of the King!

"If You Feel Like You're Unsure"

If you feel like your salvation is in question and want to know for sure, then just repeat this prayer out loud, right where you are. "Father God, forgive me for walking away from you. I repent right now, Lord, and ask Jesus back into my life. Forgive me for the wrong I have done. Now I thank you, God, for accepting me back and this time I will do everything I can not to stray from you. Thank you, God, for forgiving me. I look forward to having a great relationship with you. In Jesus name I pray, Amen."

"Final Thoughts"

I leave you with this final thought; don't fall for the "Entrapment" that the devil has laid out for you. The deceptions come in many forms, but trust me, if it feels just slightly wrong, it is wrong. Sinning and backsliding doesn't just happen overnight; it starts as something very small, a thought, a glance at something you shouldn't look at, a word, a dirty joke you laugh at, whatever it is that is just the beginning. If you resist it then, the thought, the glance, the joke, etc., it has to flee; it will not grow and you will not fail or backslide. However, if you allow that thought, that glance, that joke, etc. to grow, then you will fail and you will backslide. Pastor Wayne Friedt used to say something every Sunday morning years ago from the pulpit. He said, "What you feed grows and what you starve dies." That goes for physical, mental and spiritual, so starve out those bad thoughts and negative things in life and feed it positive and Godly things. Then the actions of your life will bear "Godly fruit", and you will not fall for the Entrapment Satan has waiting for you!

If you would like to have Ivan S Tuttle come speak at your church or organization, you can email him at
authorivanstuttle@gmail.com

www.EntrapmentHeavenandHell.com

More about Heaven, Hell and Prophesies

This section of the book was added to the Korean version back in March of 2014, after the original was written and I have been asked by many people to include it in the English version, so here it is, enjoy it and may the Holy Spirit witness to you as you read it!

More of Hell

There were things in hell that are hard to explain and even harder to describe. Once down there it is very dark, yet you can still see because you are not using your fleshly or earthly eyes, but your spiritual ones. People down there seemed to be chained up in little areas, but there were no bars or walls to prohibit them from moving; they just couldn't get out of their assigned areas.

While going through hell I met several people or souls down there as I was moving past them. Some were just everyday ordinary people, just like you and me and some were mighty people at one time, including preachers. I know people are going to wonder why preachers were in hell and I wanted to know that too while I was there and here are some of what they told me.

One man's name was Rev James Wolfe, he was from England back many years ago, at least 100 or more years from what I gathered. James told me that he regretted his sins and he asked me to tell God he was sorry for molesting those little girls. He also regretted cheating people out of food at a local market, he stole food from there and never got caught. He read his bible every day and prayed for people when asked but, he couldn't stop himself from doing those things, he never thought it mattered that much, no one was hurt he thought. Now he knows that's not true and that what he did was wrong. He hated hell.

I met a girl named Mary, didn't get her last name, but she was only 18 when she died and she couldn't understand why she was in hell. She never really believed in God, heaven or hell, but does now. Mary said she was in college and was driving home for Christmas break from college when she got hit head on by a drunk driver. She couldn't understand why God didn't forgive her because it was not her fault she died before she could accept Christ, it was the drunks fault.

Mary said she was alive for a few days in a hospital and she could hear her mother and father praying for her, but she could not do anything about it because she could not answer or move. Mary remembers them saying she was brain dead and that the doctors told her mother and father after 3 days they would take her off of life support if there were no brain waves. Mary could hear all this going on, but couldn't do anything about it. Finally on the third day, her mother and father were in her hospital room when the doctor came in and talked with her parents and everyone agreed to disconnect her. This scared Mary because she knew she wasn't dead yet and wanted to stay alive as long as possible, death scared her. Mary watched as her mother and father said goodbye to her and nodded for the nurse in the room to disconnect the life support. From what Mary was saying, I believe she was having an out of body experience or NDE - Near Death Experience. Mary said she couldn't get any air and felt like she was drowning and she said everything felt stiff like she couldn't move any part of her body, then this evil spirit came and took her to hell.

I can remember asking myself, "Why am I hearing all this from people here in hell?" I still don't have an answer for that or why this demonic beast that had a hold of me slowed down so I could hear these stories, maybe it was so I could think, now there isn't any hope of ever getting out. These people didn't seem to deserve hell, so if they can't get out, then I have no hope either. Many people screamed or yelled at me in hell and I was allowed to actually talk to several people in hell. I need to explain; as soon as I saw these people, it was less than a second that I knew these things about them and the way the communicated their stories to me was like talking without saying anything, but I heard them clear as a bell.

One other person allowed to talk to me was a person that was from Asia, but I am not sure which country. You see when you die, everyone speaks the same language but we still look like we did while alive, but it is our spirit, not our fleshly bodies, but you can still tell what a person looks like or what nationality they are, be it Black, White, Asian, Hispanic, Middle Eastern, Native American, etc. He said his name, but I am not sure how to spell it, but it seemed like it was Jung Sho He. He was a jeweler back on earth and he had a wife, two sons and a daughter. Jung believed there was no God, no heaven or hell and was shocked when he had a heart attack and died only to find out there was a hell and he was trapped there forever. He begged me to tell his wife and children if I could. At that time I only knew I was staying there forever like him.

Why were these people telling me these things, why did they think I could do anything about their situation? This didn't make sense to me at the time. I knew I was lost forever, I knew I blew my only chance to be with God in heaven. Are these people telling me these things to let me know it's hopeless?

The sights in hell are nothing like what has ever been shown to man here on earth, it was worse than any picture or movie I have ever seen trying to describe it. If you could imagine solid, jagged, rock walls with people attached by some invisible force, like being chained up and these walls go on forever, over a million miles in every direction and it is dark, it stinks, the smell of rotten flesh and garbage mixed with sulfur smell and heat so hot that your flesh would melt off its bones, that is just a little idea of what hell is like. You get there, you don't leave!

Imagine everything I described about hell and then add the torture you go through all the time, you never get a break, not even for a minute. These evil spirits are there to torture you and they get such pleasure out of it. The biggest pleasure they get is when they know you fell for their lie here on earth that they were going to take care of you, that Satan was powerful and he would protect you and give you all these wonderful treasures when you die. Yes, they love it when you are stupid enough to believe all that. People that believe in Buddha, Muhammad or other gods, they laugh at that because those gods were made up by Satan himself to satisfy man, to trick them into believing a lie so he could have them forever. They also love those that didn't believe in God while they were living, because when you go to hell it is too late, but you will believe in God then.

Our spirits look a lot like our fleshly bodies, we seem the same way, but different. This is too difficult to explain in our earthly language or too difficult for our brains to comprehend. Not everything in the spirit, in heaven or hell can be described because it can only be experienced after we leave our earthly bodies behind. With this being said, I will tell you this, hell is worse than having someone break every inch of every bone in your body, inch by inch, one bone at a time – slowly so it takes a whole month to do it. Yes, hell is worse than that. The pain that you feel when the demons are tearing you apart, but you don't come apart, you only rip and tear but you stay together. This pain is horrible.

I watched as some demons were tearing apart a young lady, maybe 18 to 20 years of age and you could tell she was a beautiful young lady at one time, yet these demons have tortured her for over 400 years and they have never stopped. No it is not something you get used to, our spirits are not like our earthly brain, we can't reason or rationalize things because we don't need to anymore, this is final.

Imagine having someone tie your hands up to two different car bumpers and the your feet at two different car bumpers and then your head tied up to another car bumper and then all at once, all the cars start pulling you apart in all different directions, but you never come apart and you can't pass out, you just suffer the pain, over and over again forever and forever. Well that would be like a vacation in hell because that's not near as bad as minor pain in hell.

I saw something else that was interesting to me in hell, I saw demons fighting over who gets to torture someone. They seemed to do this a lot, especially over people that claimed to be Christians on earth, but hid stuff about their real activities on earth. I call them "Fake Christians" because they claim to be a Christian, but their walk with God is nothing like Christ. They were only satisfied with pleasing themselves. That is one of the biggest lies Satan has Christians believing, it's okay to want and desire things, it's okay to have an affair – God will forgive you, it's okay to steal – you need the clothes or food, it's okay to cheat on that test – you studied hard and others are cheating, it's okay to spend your money on whatever you like – you don't need to give to the Lord, it's okay to satisfy yourself – everyone does, and the list goes on and on.

Demons or evil spirits cannot be described in human words or be written for you to fully understand, but they are real, they do exist. There are demons in every part of this world, remember they were thrown out of heaven where they were at one time angels or some other host of heaven, they were cast out with Lucifer or Satan. Lucifer was one of the most powerful angels at one time and he was beautiful, but when he was cast out because of his pride to want to become like God, almost a third of the heavenly hosts were cast out with him. That does not mean they were all angels because heaven has all kinds of beings in it, not just angels. Demons became so ugly and strong because they have been here on earth for thousands of years yet they still have the strength they had in heaven and they have been in hell a long time. You can't help but change due to your surroundings, even people on earth that may have been happy at one time in their life, if they marry someone and that person is miserable or grumpy all the time, the sweet person will eventually become less sweet and become grumpy and miserable too. Think about living in hell for thousands of years and knowing it will be millions and millions and billions of years and then eternity, you will never get out. That is why the demons are like they are. At one time they may have been beautiful creatures or beings living in heaven, but now doomed to hell forever, well hell has changed them.

Here is a shock for you, over one half of all people going to hell, didn't believe in hell before they died, they thought everyone would go to heaven and that hell was what we lived like on earth or what we made of life here on earth. People that believe in gods like statues, rocks, idols, Buddha, Islam, Hindu, etc. are all living a lie and when they die, they are going to be so shocked to find out that there really is a heaven and hell and there really is a God. God is not a rock or a statue, Buddha or Muhammad, He is God, the I am, the only living God that always has been and always will be, none before and none after Him! You don't have to take my word for this, or you can wait till you go to hell and then you will know what I am telling you is correct - but then it will be too late.

Future Events

Many of the things I will tell you are already in the bible, if you read it; it will confirm what I am saying. There are many things I was shown there about the future of the earth and some things I am not allowed to discuss with you or anyone. If God tells someone to seal it up and not talk about what He has shown you, then you obey, even John in Revelations was not allowed to talk about some things he saw.

Let's talk about the earthquakes I saw on earth while in heaven. Not only will earthquakes happen where they have always happened, but there are going to be great eruptions in the earth where it has laid dormant for hundreds and thousands of years. Not only earthquakes, but volcanic action as well and in areas not expected. Some of these volcanos will be so great that it will tear apart whole areas of a country. Earthquakes so strong that no one has ever recorded one like it in modern times. A 9.5 to 12.5 will be recorded in the future.

Asia will suffer in many ways it has not suffered before. Not only will buildings come down, but whole large cities will be flattened by earthquakes. May people will die by being crushed to death by the force of these earthquakes, those are the unlucky ones. The people that will suffocate after weeks of being buried alive are the ones that will have a chance to accept Jesus as their Lord before they die, but their suffering will be great. The Asian continent will have strange things happen to it, almost like plagues, where all the fish will die in a lake and no one will ever find out what caused it and rivers will turn blood red overnight. People will get sores inside their mouths and doctors will not be able to cure them. The cancer rate will climb drastically, where in other countries the progression of cancer will slow down. Children will be born with unusual birth defects and the doctors will not know what causes them. There will be born a few blonde hair children to a few Asian couples and no one will be able to explain why. There will be a great collapse of currency in China and it will affect the whole world, but it will affect all of Asia the most.

Europe will have more than its fair share of disasters too. Earthquakes will destroy places that have been around for centuries and these earthquakes are located where some have never been before. Many livestock will die of strange diseases and plague like infections that can't be controlled by antibiotics. Dams and bridges will be destroyed by earthquakes and floods. There will be times of extreme drought and then extreme rains that seem to never end raining sometimes for forty five (45) days straight. European countries will start to not trust the other European countries and they will withdraw from each other. Natural disasters will happen throughout all Europe.

Russia will suffer in different ways; there will be things that happen over the skies of Russia that will make people repent because they are so unusual. *Not only will the earth shake in Russia, but it will open up holes in places, unusual types never seen before.* Russia will become boastful for a time, seeming to be the big bear again, but that will collapse because the people will not want to be ruled like that again. The Russian people are proud, they take pride in their ways, but they no longer want war, they want to live in peace. They are good people and they have learned to live with hardships and live a difficult life compared to most other standards of the world and they have not only survived, but have proven they are a strong people.

Sweden, Norway, Denmark have always been a place of refuge, but not in the coming years, they will see disasters they have never dealt with before. Some of their own people will start to commit horrendous crimes like they have never seen and families will turn against families. War will break out between them and other parts of the world. They will no longer be a safe haven.

South America will see some of the worst earthquakes and the most frequent for a time. Usually the earthquakes are related to the western half, but the eastern side will have some as well now. Countries like Ecuador, Columbia and Chile will be a hot spot for earthquakes. Crime in Brazil will climb higher than ever before; there will be violence that the country of Brazil like it has never seen in this quantity before. In the jungles and rain forests, there will be fires that seem like they will never stop. In Rio de Janeiro you will see buildings and large statues that will fall as the earth continues to shift.

India will suffer greatly as the earth shakes and rattles all who live there, no one in India or Pakistan will escape from this terror. Some will die from this, others from starvation and yet others from robbers and looters. The women will be rapped and ravished, forced into horrible situations such as sex slaves, this includes young girls as young as six years old. This not only happens in India, but parts of Indonesia too. The types of plagues caused by the dead bodies lying in the alleyways and in the streets will kill thousands upon thousands in that part of the world. There will be no food for almost half of these countries, India and Pakistan in those days.

Africa will become divided between Christians and non-Christians and there will be horrible wars. The people of the Muslim faith will try to kill all Christians in that area because they feel they must rule all of Africa. They fill people's heads with lies about a better afterlife and they promise them things they cannot deliver, but by the time they found out they have been tricked or fooled, it is too late. The stench from dying bodies there will be horrible. Diseases will run rampant in all of Africa and because of their sinful desires, the diseases will spread even faster than anyone could have expected. Men, women and children alike will be infected and die.

Mexico and Central America will suffer much like South America except there will be a good size volcano to erupt in Mexico. The earthquakes in Mexico will kill more because of landslides caused by the earthquakes and the volcano erupting. People will die from starvation in parts of northern and central Mexico. People in Central America and Mexico will have diseases that give flu like symptoms, but the fevers will be over 105 degrees and the people will die, especially children.

North America, including the United States and Canada, will receive its fair share of earthquakes and volcanos erupting. There will be a massive volcano eruption in the United States that will affect the whole world's climate and this was not something expected. The volcano will erupt out of Wyoming, in the Yellowstone area and it will be so massive that for hundreds of miles around, nothing will be left standing and the toxic cloud it will produce and the ash cloud will cover most of Canada and two thirds of the United States. It will change the global climate and even people in the tropics will feel freezing temperatures for the first time. This is not all that will happen there, the sin and corruption that has been so blatant will increase until the time that God has set aside for the people to revolt as one. When this time comes there will be a major shift in how this government is run. The people will take back their governments and the liberal policies will be overturned and God will be put back into their government and schools. They will repent!

Australia and New Zealand will not be spared by the earthquakes and natural disasters. New Zealand will get hit especially hard on the amount of earthquakes but it will not see the 9.5 or higher earthquakes, it will have many of them though. Australia will suffer more by weather related occurrences than anything else. The extreme heat and cold will grip that nation and there will be pestilence over that country that has never been seen before. Flies and gnats will fill the air and make the skies seem dark during the day.

There is a sound like no other sound heard before on earth that people from every nation will hear, it is the sound of the earth moaning. This sound will travel all around the earth and people will hear it and try to explain it, they will even record it, but no one can explain what it really is and where it came from, but you will know it is the earth moaning!

No nation, no continent, no state or no city will escape this wrath, the earth will seem to turn on itself and cause many to believe the end is near, but these things must happen. Some of you reading this book will see these things occur, while some will just see the beginning of it. The warning light is on, the siren is sounding, take heed and be warned, pray. These things can be changed through prayer, just as Moses changed God's mind not to kill the Israelites, so you can change the course of events through prayer, but some natural disasters will have to happen because not everyone will take the warnings and they will battle against God.

Now this is what happens because of these things. People will turn their back on the ways in which sin was ruling their life; they will know that there is a God. Yes, there will be wars and rumors of wars, but there will be peace among those who believe. Those that really love the Lord will not feel abandoned, but will feel the Love God has for them.

What Heaven Was Like

This is going to be difficult because nothing we have on earth compares. In heaven there is no darkness, no shadows of any kind. Imagine light being everywhere, you walk under a tree and it is just as light as standing out in direct sunlight. You look up through the leaves of the tree and there are no shadows between the leaves, the light engulfs everything. Because of this, colors look different in heaven, more vibrant and pure. Nothing on earth can compare to the light or colors in heaven and our earthly minds cannot explain or comprehend what it looks like.

Some people say the streets are gold, but the reality is, it's difficult to say what they are made of because everything there is so shinny and bright. The buildings there seemed very white to me as if they were some kind of white marble. Now inside the houses or mansions the light is just a bright on the inside as it is outside, so difficult to explain. As I walked around in heaven I was looking everywhere including down at my feet and the streets I walked on just glowed like a high gloss gold, but it didn't feel like gold, it was actually soft feeling. I won't even begin to tell you what the grass or flowers looked like, my brain cannot find the words to describe them, but I can tell you that walking on the grass barefoot was a rush, the grass was so soft – like walking on a cloud!

You can float in heaven, all you do is pick your feet up and think about floating and you do, it's effortless. There is no top that I could see in heaven, so if you wanted to, you could soar as high as any eagle or airplane here on earth, but in heaven, it's not a big deal, it's like walking. Every movement you make is effortless, you never get tired and you can always be on the move. Oh how I wish that were true on earth! Sigh.

When you look towards the center, or what I thought was the center of heaven, you see this light that surpasses anything you have ever seen. The light has warmth like the feeling of honey flowing all over you, without the stickiness. You can see forever and hear things that you could never hear on earth. Can you imagine a place where no fear exists? No sickness, no sorrow, no sadness, not any form of depression of any kind, everyone was happy all the time!

I know I saw some of the people out of the bible moving around in heaven because you instantly know things, like who someone is, without anyone saying a thing to you. I know I saw Elisha, John the Baptist, Matthew and Luke. I did not speak to any of them, I just saw them going about heaven, you see, I wasn't supposed to be there yet, or at least be allowed to stay there. The angel stayed with me wherever I went and I didn't go too far from the gate. As I mentioned before, you could see forever and your vision is perfect and everything is crystal clear, seeing these men was not that difficult. I saw many other people too but we did not talk. It was so great not to have to talk to someone and ask them their name, you just knew it, even if they walked by you. There is one name that sticks out and I don't know why, she was not anyone from the bible days or anyone I knew about before, her name was Esther Remington. I hope someone reading this will know something about her or why it was important to remember her name. She died when she was old, but she looked so young now and she was a very loving woman on earth. I believe Esther was from California and had died a few years before I arrived in heaven, maybe late 1960's or early 1970's.

Once you have been to heaven, not experienced it in a vision or dream, but actually been there, you have a different outlook on life than anyone else. You see things differently and understand things others cannot. Your passion for life and people is magnified when you come back and you have an understanding and compassion you never had before. You know how important it is to talk to people and win souls for the Lord, because after you die, it is too late.

I was given several gifts in heaven, but the most awesome gift any of us can ever have and the only gift you can take with you to heaven is, Love!

Made in the USA
San Bernardino, CA
29 May 2020